THE FIFE COASTAL PATH

The Official Guide

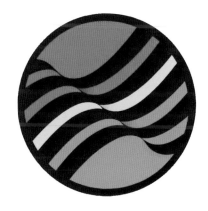

FIFE COAST AND COUNTRYSIDE TRUST

THE FIFE COASTAL PATH

The Official Guide

www.fifecoastalpath.co.uk

First published in June 2012 by Fife Coast and Countryside Trust,
The Harbourmaster's House, Hot Pot Wynd, Dysart, KY1 2TQ, Fife.

ISBN: 978-0-9572346-0-4

A CIP catalogue record for this book is available from the British Library.
All information published in this book was correct at time of research and
publication. Fife Coast and Countryside Trust cannot be held responsible for any
inaccuracies or errors caused by information changing since the publication of
this edition.

Photographs: Caroline Trotter and Christine McGuinness
Cover photograph: David Anderson
Back cover photograph: Matt Miller
Photograph of Jack Vettriano: Richard Kalina

Printed and bound by Bell and Bain, Thornliebank, Glasgow.

ACKNOWLEDGEMENTS

We would like to extend our thanks to the following people and organisations who have helped with the production of this book:

The Mary Leishman Foundation whose financial donation has helped us print this guide.

Caroline Trotter and Christine McGuinness for their wonderful pictures which have brought our text to life.

Mr D.G. Anderson, the winner of our photographic competition, whose entry is on the front cover of this guide.

Matt Miller for the back cover photograph.

Kate Hogarth for her insight into Fife's history and her interpretation in our `Did You Know' sections.

Our staff for their continued commitment to the Fife Coastal Path. A special mention must go to Derek, Stewart, Deirdre, Ranald and Kate for writing their sections of the book and to our dedicated path maintenance team.

Thank you to the landowners along the path. Without their commitment and support the Coastal Path experience would not be possible.

And finally, to you the reader, thank you for choosing the Fife Coastal Path. We hope you love it as much as we do.

CONTENTS

INTRODUCTION

THE Fife Coastal Path is one of the best ways of exploring the Kingdom of Fife. The 117-mile walk takes you on a journey through countryside, villages and towns where you will experience some of the best that Fife has to offer. Just follow the Waymarker to keep you on the right track.

The Kingdom was home to Scotland's capital Dunfermline for six centuries and has always been at the heart of the nation's history. The evidence is there in its wealth of castles, cathedrals, harbours and other places of historic interest, many of which can be found along the Path.

Fife is a peninsula, sitting between Edinburgh in the south and Dundee in the north. It is surrounded by the North Sea, the Firth of Forth and the Firth of Tay. Despite its relatively small size, barely 50 miles at its widest point, Fife has been named the number one destination for outdoor recreation in Scotland for four consecutive years.

The Fife Coastal Path is managed, maintained and promoted by Fife Coast and Countryside Trust. We are an environmental charity based in the historic Harbourmaster's House in Dysart. You will learn more about Dysart and the many picturesque coastal villages as our Rangers guide you along the path, chapter by chapter.

Since our Trust Patron, Jim Leishman MBE officially opened the completed path in 2003, it has always had a reputation as one of the finest long distance routes in Scotland and is recognised by Scottish Natural Heritage as one of Scotland's Great Trails www.scotlandsgreattrails.org. We were also delighted the path was voted runner up in the UK Coastal Path Awards by the readers of Coast magazine.

This book has been written by Fife Coast and Countryside Trust's Rangers, who between them have decades of experience of the Coastal Path. They will give you unique insights into the culture and natural heritage along the path as well as letting you know about some of the hidden gems along the way.

The chapters within this guide have been planned so that the path can be explored from south to north. This often means you have a favourable wind to help you and in easy-to-walk sections, making it suitable for many different types of users. However, the path can of course be explored from the other direction.

Whether you plan to discover the entire coastline of Fife in one go, or do it in bite-sized chunks, this guide will open your eyes to a new walking experience.

We hope you enjoy this book and also have a great time on our Coastal Path. We would be delighted to hear about your experiences and to share your photographs.

Please feel free to email us at ask.us@fifecountryside.co.uk.

Happy walking!

FOREWORD

THE Fife Coastal Path means the world to me. It's my own little piece of heaven on earth.

Back in 2008, my wife Mary and I had planned to spend our summer holidays walking from St Andrews back to Dunfermline. Sadly, it wasn't to be, as she was taken from us before we got to share the experience.

But some friends came to me and suggested we do the walk in her memory – and so began The Mary Leishman Foundation, a charity that has since raised more than £400,000.

We've had golf tournaments in Spain, dinners, dances, pub quizzes and karaoke nights. We've had Sir Alex Ferguson live on stage to an audience of 1,200. What none of us ever forget though is that all of it stems from our very first Dander for Mary along the winding miles of this very special piece of the Kingdom.

Every one of the dozens who join us on the Dander each summer has their own favourite spots, little gems that make their hearts sing or where they just stop and stare in wonder at the beauty of the sea, the skies, the sand and the rocks.

Me? I love the whole thing, every step we take. And then comes the night when we stop off at the likes of Anstruther, Elie or Aberdour for the kind of fun that makes the Coastal Path even more memorable.

It was an enormous honour when I was asked to become a Patron of the Fife Coast and Countryside Trust – and it's with huge pride that wherever I go around the world, I spread the word of what a wonderful job all those involved in it do.

That's why I'm delighted to see this guide produced because the more visitors who get to share in the magic of my beloved county, the better.

See you on the trail soon...
Provost of Fife Jim Leishman MBE.

WHAT FAMOUS FIFERS SAY...

'Fife is blessed to have both wonderful countryside and a beautiful coastline. We are also fortunate to have the Fife Coast and Countryside Trust whose dedicated work and commitment has given us a fantastic coastal path that both locals and visitors can enjoy. I hope that they will continue with this wonderful work for years to come.'

Dougray Scott

'I like coming back because this is the place that made me who I am. In Scotland, people talk about 'ma ain folk', my own people, and these are 'ma ain folk' around here, where I grew up.

'During the summer, the whole game of picking up girls was played out during the day. There was the bingo, the fairground, the promenade. I don't know how many summers I spent by the Waltzers, looking at the girls. The game was being played around the clock. You know the game of life and love is played out on the beaches because that's where you go to fall in love. It is a place where courtship takes place.

'It was a lovely place to grow up and I think people don't realise just how breathtaking the beaches are – it's 45 minutes away on the train from Edinburgh and yet you feel like you are in a faraway land. Leven beach is famously long and is not only stunningly beautiful, but there is also always lots going on. I think you can tell how much I love the beaches from my early paintings such as The Billy Boys and of course, The Singing Butler. People just seemed to respond to the imagery and the romance of couples dancing on the sands.

'What I like is the fact that you can see anyone from different walks of life here on Leven Beach – families, couples and teens just starting out together. I have a studio in Nice, France where I work from because the light there is just incredible, but nothing beats Leven for me.

'I'm very indebted to this part of the world because it was what formed the man and gave me such a reservoir of material to draw from. There is something about being Scottish that makes you want to hang on to your roots.

'When the plane comes up past North Berwick and turns, you see the Fife coastline quite clearly, and that does make you feel a certain pride. Its beauty still amazes me and I can't help but start to remember the past. My paintings may have moved on from beach scenes, but the memories of days gone by still keep me going.'

Jack Vettriano

'The Fife Coastal Path is a wonderful asset enjoyed by Fifers and visitors to the Kingdom. Sarah and I, along with our two sons, have been exploring the path over the past year and have had great fun doing so. Although we have yet to walk some of the sections, our favourite spot so far is the stretch around Aberdour.

'Aberdour is a picturesque village that nestles between two amazing beaches, Silver Sands and Black Sands.

'Silver Sands, one of Fife's Blue Flag beaches, is a great place to take a break from walking and to explore the numerous rock pools in search of hermit crabs and shrimps – and if you are lucky you might spot one or more of the seals that live on Inchcolm Island.

'We are, as a family, looking forward to exploring other sections of the path as I am sure these will bring further enjoyment and discovery.'

Gordon Brown MP

TO HELP YOU ON YOUR WAY

We would like to remind you of a few points that will help you enjoy your voyage of discovery along our wonderful coast.

Remember to follow the Scottish Outdoor Access Code. Further details can be found at www.outdooraccess-scotland.com or in Chapter 16 of this guide.

● **Always keep to the designated path, avoid straying into crops and leave gates as you find them.**

● If the path crosses or is close to a golf course please take extra care.

● **Always remember to be prepared for the changing weather in Scotland.**

● If you are walking with man's best friend, your dog, keep it under control and be aware of livestock.

● **Some of the Coastal Path can only be walked at low tide. Where possible we have offered high tide alternatives. If you are in doubt, please check tide times before you start your walk.**

The Fife Coastal Path has a series of Welcome Ports along the entire route. The aim of a Welcome Port is to provide key facilities for users of the path such as information, toilet facilities and a chance to fill up your water bottle. Look out for the Welcome Port logo in their window or check the business listings section at the end of each chapter of this book.

Useful Contacts

Fife Coast and Countryside Trust:	01592 656080
Local Coast Guard:	01333 450666
Scottish Society for the Prevention of Cruelty to Animals (SSPCA):	03000 999999
Traveline:	0871 200 22 33
Fife Council Access Officer:	01592 583239
NHS 24:	08454 242424
Luggage Transport:	01333 311184
Visit Scotland:	01334 472021
Exploring Fife:	01592 891174

To check public toilet opening times check our website www.fifecoastalpath.co.uk.

Fife Coast and Countryside Trust is a registered charity. If you would like to support us and help to protect the Fife Coastal Path for future generations, why not send us a donation in one of the following ways.

By cheque: payable to Fife Coast and Countryside Trust
Send to: The Harbourmaster's House
Hot Pot Wynd
Dysart
Fife, KY1 2TQ

By SMS/text: Simply text your donation to 70070. For example if you wished to donate £10 then text FCCT12 £10

You will receive a confirmation text to tell you that your donation has been received. If you are a UK taxpayer, don't forget that you can Gift Aid your donation.

Online: www.justgiving.com/fifecoastandcountrysidetrust/donate
or simply scan the box to the right if you have a smartphone.

Thank you for your support and helping keep our Coastal Path special for future generations.

KEY TO THE COASTAL PATH MAPS

Fife Coastal Path Key

▬	Easy path with flat terrain	⇄	Railway Station
▬	Unmade path and rough terrain	🚌	Bus Station
▬	Remote path with rough terrain	▶	Bus Stop
▬	Road	▶	Hail & Ride
▨	Cycle Route	P	Car Park
▮▮▮▮	Railway	🚻	Toilets *(subject to seasonal closure)*
● Welcome Port	Welcome Port	▪▪▪▪	Low Tide Route
☀	View Point	▪▪▪▪	High Tide Route
🎋	Picnic Area		

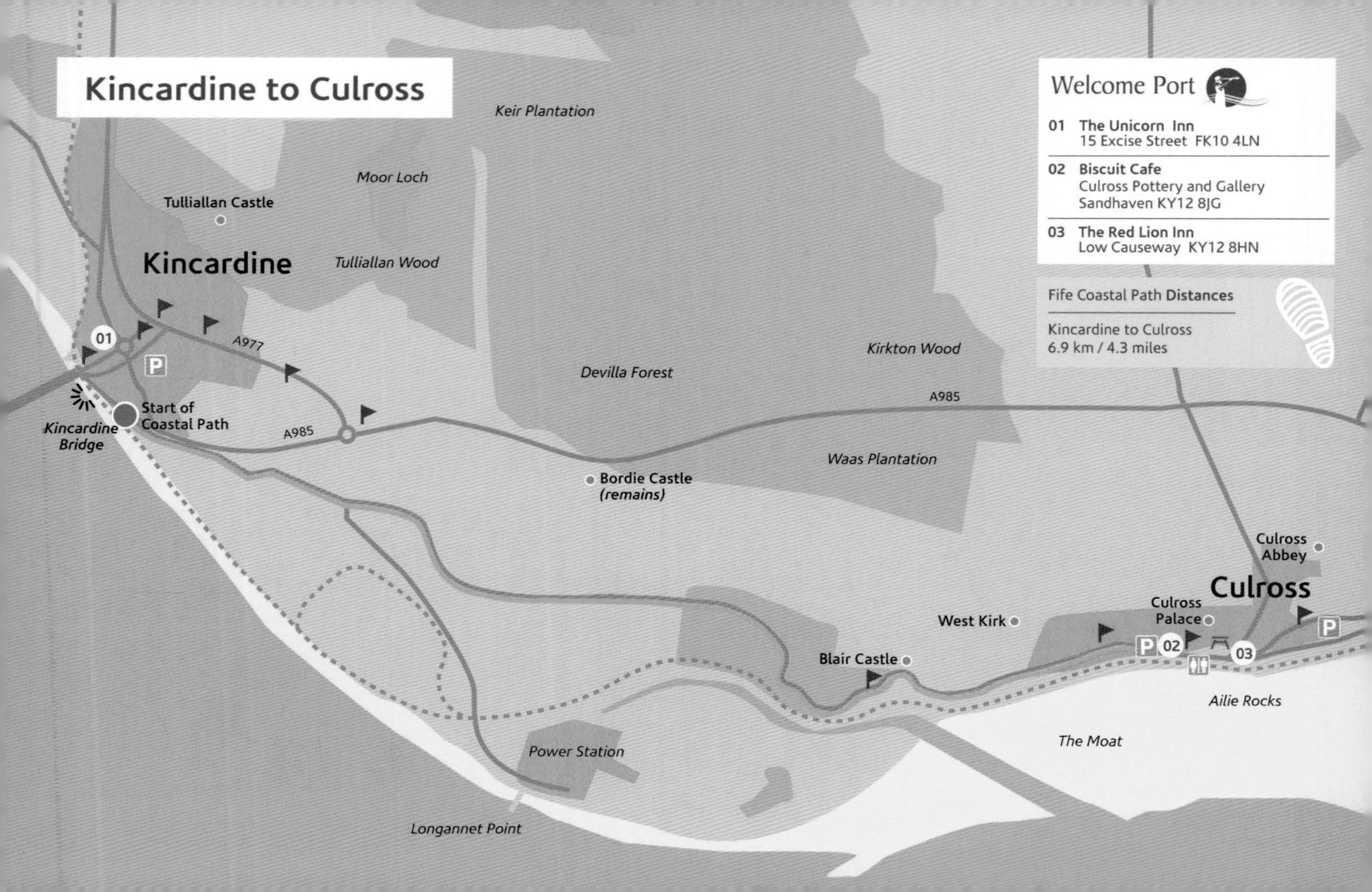

Kincardine to Culross

Welcome Port

01 **The Unicorn Inn**
15 Excise Street FK10 4LN

02 **Biscuit Cafe**
Culross Pottery and Gallery
Sandhaven KY12 8JG

03 **The Red Lion Inn**
Low Causeway KY12 8HN

Fife Coastal Path Distances

Kincardine to Culross
6.9 km / 4.3 miles

Keir Plantation

Tulliallan Castle

Moor Loch

Tulliallan Wood

Kincardine

A977

A985

01

P

Start of
Coastal Path

Kincardine
Bridge

Kirkton Wood

A985

Devilla Forest

Waas Plantation

Bordie Castle
(remains)

West Kirk

Blair Castle

Power Station

Longannet Point

Culross

Culross
Abbey

Culross
Palace

P 02

03

P

The Moat

Ailie Rocks

CHAPTER ONE

KINCARDINE TO CULROSS EAST

I became a Countryside Ranger five years ago hoping that I could make a difference to people's enjoyment of the great outdoors by promoting public awareness of wildlife, landscape and history in our wonderful corner of the country.

My favourite bit of the coastal path is the stretch from Torryburn Ness to Crombie Point – it puts you right on the high water mark with great views of our wildlife and hidden botanical gems.

This section of the Fife Coastal Path is 4.3 miles long (6.9 km) and easy walking. It starts at Kincardine Bridge and passes the power station at Longannet, then takes you along the main cycle route 76 before passing through Culross with its rich historic heritage. It ends at the car park on the east side of Culross.

Countryside Ranger
Derek Abbott

This is the first section of what I hope will be a pleasant and diverse exploration of the coastal fringe of Fife, a golden crown befitting the oldest Kingdom in Britain.

The path starts at the older of Kincardine's two road bridges. It is worth taking a few minutes to view what was, at one time, the longest road bridge in Britain. The bridge was built in 1936 and the centre span would swing round to allow ships to pass through.

A vacuum flask is a good idea on the journey and as it was invented by James Dewar, a son of Kincardine, it will serve as a constant warm souvenir as you make your way along.

Cast your eye southeast over the far bank and you will see an area of mudflats that are actually called skinflats. Mudflats are an important aspect of the inner Forth estuary and line both banks, creating some of the richest feeding areas for waders in Britain.

As you walk along this and many of the western sections of the coastal path you will see various flocks of waders and sea birds moving from area to area. One species that you will see lots of is oystercatcher, a large stocky black and white wading bird. It is believed they were blessed by St Bride for saving her life and hence the white cross on their backs. These birds have a connection with Tulliallan Castle, now a police college that is located on the north side of Kincardine. The

You will see lots of oystercatchers on this part of the Fife Coastal Path

College motto `BI GLIC-BI GLIC' is said to be the cry of the oystercatcher and when translated from Gaelic means, `Be wise – be circumspect'. So, with your flask and oystercatchers for company, you will always have a constant reminder of where your walk along the Fife Coastal Path started.

The path follows the line of the A985 and the banking separating the path from the road is worth keeping an eye on as it is full of wild flowers with plenty of mayweed, trefoil, knapweed and scabious, all great for our bumblebees. All six of our most common species can be seen here. As you meander along the path you will come to a corner where Kincardine Community Council have kindly placed a bench. When you reach this point, turn and look back to get a better view of the bridge.

As you approach Inch House look out for the mature sycamore trees and the walled garden to the west side…but the best bit is the horse chestnut tree just on the field margin. If the season is right then there's plenty of opportunity to collect conkers and a game should be on. You are never too old for a game of conkers! And if you have not got string then here's a tip. We used to use our laces. I remember my dad and I making and playing conkers as we walked the paths and woods of Fife – a pleasure shared.

The wood mill at Inch Farm should now come into view and with it your first glimpse of Longannet Power Station behind. This is a good place to stop and view the station. Power generation and coal have been a major factor in the industrialisation of the area. Kincardine itself is built on reclaimed land and was at one time sandwiched between two power stations. I personally like to use the chimney as a beacon as it can be seen for miles and is a good reference of how far you have travelled on your journey around Fife's Coastal Path.

The road comes to a staggered junction and care should be taken, as it can get very busy at certain times of the day. Your journey continues to the next section that follows along the main road as it heads towards Culross.

The short hill ends with a pretty little cottage called West Lodge. Look at the path margin opposite the cottage and here you should find large-leafed plants called butterbur, flowering early in spring. The path descends slightly into a little row of houses called Longannet Cottages. I find the name strange as the houses are two storeys high and terraced... but what's in a name?

Just past the cottages the path is bordered with a fine row of mature sycamore with a hedge behind, all very pretty. Watch out for some concealed entrances on this section. Sycamore is excellent for honeybees and sycamore honey is lovely, worth tasting if you ever get the chance. Proceed along the path until you come to the next field on your right where you should find two large pylons – wait until you are between both and you will be rewarded with one of the best views of the power station as the main grid output lines flank you.

The field on the opposite side of the road on occasions can be full of various coloured garden roses, row upon row and it is quite visually impressive as well as fragrant. This contrasts with the path margins that are full of mayweeds and poppies.

The path now skirts a little wooded area just at the entrance to Sands Farm. As you leave the woods the two fields on your right are a favourite haunt of pink-footed geese and curlews during the autumn and winter months.

Looking over the fields you may just see an area of standing water. These are Longannet's Ash Lagoons and are home to a large gull colony. Watch out for the white painted telegraph pole in the middle of the path! Follow the path onwards past the buildings on the right until you come to a wooded area with a high green metal fence. A beech hedge will obscure the fence eventually, but until it does, look into this wood as I have often watched and listened to green woodpeckers here.

I once had a weird experience with a woodpecker. It was springtime and I decided to go for a short walk just before going to a wedding reception, so I was dressed in my finest Highland dress complete with leather sporran. As I walked along I became convinced that a woodpecker was following me as it repeatedly came in and out of view. This puzzled me for a

The butterbur plant flowers in early spring

little while until it dawned on me that my sporran was making a drumming noise as the three leather tassels tapped on the sporran. The bird must have assumed there was a strange-shaped woodpecker in Highland dress lurking about. So if you want to attract woodpeckers get yourself a leather sporran and go for a walk in the woods. But be warned though, you may get strange looks from fellow walkers!

The path gently descends until it reaches Scottish Power's access gate where the path is marked with a couple of white bollards. There's also a disused quarry on the opposite side of the road. Here, while looking over the gate I once spotted a pied wagtail – a delightful, small, long-tailed and rather sprightly black and white bird – getting really agitated and making a right racket, but totally ignoring me even although I was only about ten feet away. Then I saw the reason why. A weasel came out of the long grass. The wagtail dived at the weasel and it in turn was jumping in the air trying to catch the wagtail. Then the weasel stopped, looked me straight in the eye and scurried away into the grass, again pursued by the wagtail.

Weasels must be some of the boldest little creatures we will ever come across – do they really know what size they are?

The path skirts the edge of the wood before rejoining the road and follows the road around the next couple of corners. Eventually you will come across a white painted wall up on the far bank. This area has been cleared of sycamore trees so that the old orchard can be recreated and is a project to watch if you plan to repeat your visit to the area. Blair Castle sits above the orchard and unfortunately out of sight.

An old mansion built in 1840 on the same site of the old castle is now used as a convalescent home for miners. As you leave the orchard area behind keep an eye out for the marsh area on your side of the road. Meadowsweet abounds on the marsh perimeter giving off that heady smell when it is in bloom. This is a great plant for wine, although I think this patch is a bit too close to the traffic for wine use. The area of reeds is a good place to see reed buntings, sedge warblers and reed warblers, but sometimes you need to use your ears to find where they are.

Follow the path and just as it turns off to follow the railway line look back where the Fife Council and European funding sign is and you will see the chimney of Longannet marking where you have come from. Now as you turn the corner you get your first glimpse of the Forth rail and road bridges. The path runs alongside the railway line and actually runs on top of the pipes carrying the pulverised fuel ash from Longannet Power Station to the lagoons at Low Valleyfield. The path is long and straight bordering the nature reserve with good views across the Forth to Bo`ness and Grangemouth. If you are lucky the occasional steam train travels along the line and passes within a few yards of you. This is really nostalgic for me as I can remember as a boy going visiting relatives by steam train.

A bird's-eye view of the Torry Bay Nature Reserve

The tide will play a large part in what can be seen. If it is high, watch out for roosting black-headed gulls, sandwich terns and your constant companions oystercatchers roosting on the rocks. If it is low then often all you will see in the distance are little specks that are the birds feeding at the water margin.

Before you get into Culross you will pass a large salt marsh on your left. Here again, this is a good place for warblers and reed buntings.

Continue on the path until you are opposite the Town Hall and Palace. As you look around a real mismatch of environments can be seen. You have Longannet Power Station behind you, the lagoon area up in front, the road and rail bridges in the far distance, plumes of white steam coming from Grangemouth over the Forth, a nature reserve along the beach area and the old historic buildings frozen in time right beside you. All these things combine to give you one of the most fascinating areas in Scotland.

Your journey ends just a few hundred yards onwards at the car park on the east side of Culross. Please take time out to explore Culross, as there is so much to see. I have deliberately avoided talking about its historical features as that would take up a book on its own.

Did You Know?
Bees

IF YOU'RE a regular in the great outdoors, it's all too easy to become a bit too accustomed to 'regular' wildlife: flocks of playful sparrows, squawking gulls, and busy bees are common sights that can be overlooked in the search for something just a little more elusive, or for a glimpse of something rare.

Worryingly, sightings of bumblebees could too become a rarity as several bumblebee species are declining and two are already extinct within the UK. The effect of a declining bumblebee population cannot be underestimated. For there is nothing humble about the bumblebee. These tiny creatures are worth a fortune to our economy, in fact the Bumblebee Conservation Society places the value of Europe's bumblebees at a staggering €14.2 billion. As our chief pollinators, bees are essential to the growing of a vast amount of the food that we eat: and some estimates go so far as to suggest that the work of bees is essential to as much as 80% of our food. And with bumblebees able to withstand wetter and colder conditions than their honeybee counterparts, they are particularly crucial as pollinators in Scotland. Without the work of bumblebees, supermarket shelves would change as all sorts of crops and plants such as tomatoes and soft fruits would become increasingly rare and therefore much more expensive too.

There are a number of reasons why bumblebee and honeybee populations are in decline. The term 'colony collapse disorder' has been gaining increasing publicity in recent years – particularly in the USA – and describes the scenario where the adult honeybees disappear from a hive and the colony is lost.

Although this term is relatively new, it is not thought that the phenomenon that it describes is recent – just that it has not been seen or recorded on such a scale before. According to the International Bee Research Association, the reasons behind this decline are both uncertain and varied. They range from increasing urban development, changes in farming practices, changes in pests and diseases, to the increased use of pesticides and the impacts of a changing climate too. Although much more research is required into the loss of bee species, there are some more obvious root causes.

Scottish Natural Heritage states that: `The main threat to bumblebees and other bees is the loss of nectar-rich perennial herbaceous vegetation. This habitat is disappearing largely because of intensification of land use, heavy summer grazing, reduction in rotation period, fertilisation, adoption of silage or monoculture grass crops, and loss of uncultivated herb-rich borders and verges.` Put simply, the places where bees would traditionally thrive are disappearing.

It's not all doom and gloom though. Awareness of the plight of the bumblebee is growing and things can and are being done. The UK Biodiversity Action Plan has identified six bee species as being particularly at risk and has put them on its priority list. This important classification is used to influence actions at all levels, including statutory interventions, as well as providing a driver for comprehensive information and monitoring.

LOCAL BUSINESSES

KINCARDINE

Food and beverage

The Unicorn Inn Restaurant and Coffee Shop, 15 Excise Street, FK10 4LN Tel: 01259 739129 www.theunicorn.co.uk (Welcome Port)

The Auld Hoose Public House, 26 Forth Street, Kincardine, FK10 4LX. Tel: 01259 731260

Garvies Lounge Bar, 2 Elphinstone Street, Kincardine, FK10 4ND. Tel: 01259 739015

The Bridge Bar, 7 Keith Street, Kincardine, FK10 4ND Tel: 01259 730231

The Co-operative Supermarket, 25 High Street, Kincardine, FK10 4RJ. Tel: 01259 730240

The Village Store, 22-24 High Street, Kincardine, FK10 4RJ. Tel: 01259 731207

Bayne's the Bakers, 29a High Street, Kincardine, FK10 4RJ. Tel: 01259 761129

Village Tandoori Takeaway, 14 Elphinstone Street, Kincardine, FK10 4RH. Tel: 01259 731701

King Valley Takeaway, 13 Elphinstone Street, Kincardine, FK10 4RH. Tel: 01259 730404

The Spice of Life Takeaway, 19-23 High Street, Kincardine, FK10 4RJ. Tel: 01259 730324

Ilaro's Pizza Bar, 3 High Street, Kincardine, FK10 4RJ. Tel: 01259 730455

Banks

ATM, School Street, Kincardine, FK10 4PT

Medical

Co-op Pharmacy, 31 High Street, Kincardine, FK10 4RJ. Tel: 01259 730446

NHS 24, 08454 24 24 24

Post Office

Kincardine Post Office, 9-11 Keith Street, FK10 4ND. Tel: 01259 730221

CULROSS

Accommodation

St. Mungo's B&B, Low Causeway, Culross, KY11 3JG. Tel: 01383 882102

Food and Beverage

Biscuit Café, Sandhaven, Culross, KY12 8JG. Tel: 01383 882176, www.culrosspottery.com

The Red Lion Inn, Low Causeway, Culross, KY12 8HN. Tel: 01383 880225, www.theredlionculross.co.uk (Welcome Port)

Post Office

Culross Post Office, Low Causeway, Culross, KY12 3JG. Tel: 01383 880298

Tourist attractions

Culross Abbey, Kirk Street, Culross, KY12 8JD. Tel: 0131 668 8800

Culross Palace, West Green, Culross, KY12 8JH. Tel: 01383 880358

Culross Pottery and Gallery, Sandhaven, Culross, KY12 8JG. Tel: 01383 882176, www.culrosspottery.com

Culross East to Torryburn Ness

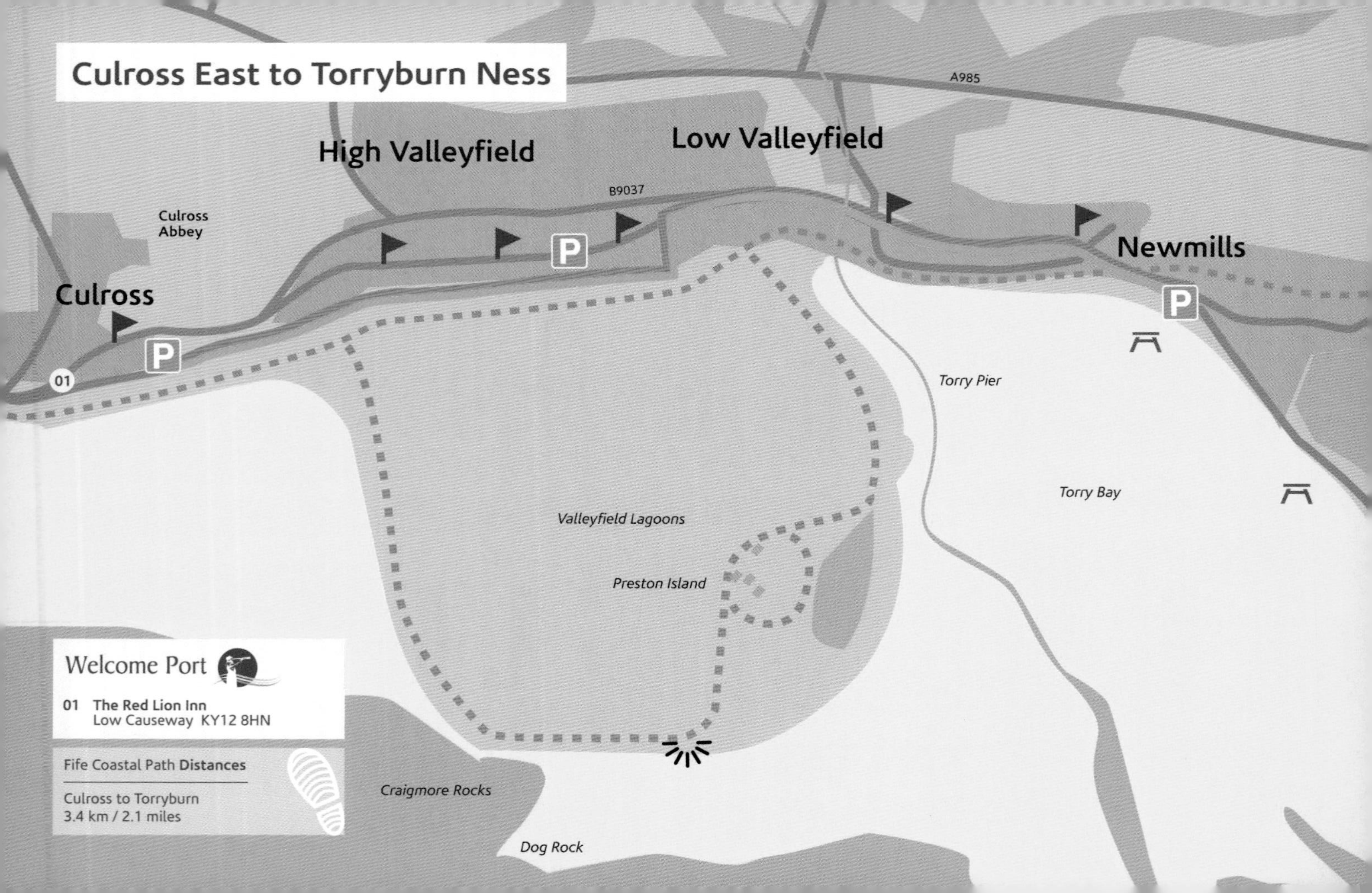

Newmills

A985

Low Valleyfield

High Valleyfield

B9037

Culross

Culross Abbey

Torry Pier

Torry Bay

Valleyfield Lagoons

Preston Island

Dog Rock

Craigmore Rocks

01

Welcome Port

01 The Red Lion Inn
Low Causeway KY12 8HN

Fife Coastal Path Distances

Culross to Torryburn
3.4 km / 2.1 miles

CHAPTER TWO

CULROSS EAST TO TORRYBURN NESS

THIS section of the Fife Coastal Path is 2.1 miles long (3.4 km) and again is easy walking. It takes in the main nature reserve of Torry Bay, the Ash Lagoons and, with a short detour, the historic industrial heritage of Preston Island. The path goes through the village of Newmills before finishing at the Ness Car Park in Torryburn.

Your journey starts at the car park at the east end of Culross village and you access the path at the south end of the car park. An information panel on the Torry Bay Nature Reserve, Culross and the Coastal Path is sited within and adjacent to the car park. As soon as you are on the path, stop for a second and look north, where you will see the view is dominated by The Abbey House, which contrasts strongly with the Palace, at Culross.

The Abbey House front was built in 1608 by Edward Bruce (Lord Kinloss) and was home to Admiral Thomas Cochrane in 1775. We are now leaving an area rich in cultural heritage and heading into more modern land creation. Look south

Abbey House at Culross, above and Culross Palace, below

from your viewpoint and you are looking over Torry Bay Nature Reserve to Grangemouth. I sometimes wonder what a strange mix all these aspects are and yet they all work together in this landscape.

Start walking along the path and within 150 yards you will come across a little area of salt marsh on your left. This area floods on high tides and it is worth stopping for a second to see if you can catch a glimpse of reed and sedge warblers although often it is your ears that will alert you of their presence first.

Head along the path and cross the railway level crossing. Take a minute to sit on the bench and look at the mudflats if the tide is out.

Watch out for shelduck and curlews that haunt this corner of the reserve. You are now faced with a choice of either going straight along the main path or taking a detour to the right for Preston Island.

Both routes have something to offer the walker and I will give a short description of the features and points of interest to help you make your choice.

MAIN PATH

The main path continues on through an area of woodland and skirts the north side of the meadow and Ash Lagoons.

All this area is reclaimed land and is where the ash from Longannet Power Station is deposited and then landscaped over. Within a few yards you will come across a small path leading to the right that skirts the meadow and wooded area to rejoin the main path a few hundred yards along. I prefer to take this route; however, you can stick to the main path if you wish.

Off on your right hand side is the meadow area that is just a small portion of the 220 hectares of reclaimed land. As you walk along ponder on the potential of what this site could become as an area of wild flower meadow, especially when you consider this meadow is only a small fraction of the whole area of reclaimed land.

Hopefully you will be passing in the months when the sea buckthorn is in fruit and there is a large stand of the orange berries in the meadow. For those who can positively identify this plant take a few berries and try them, or better still, get someone else to try them. I love to watch the shock as the tart berries suck their cheeks together. They are, however, extremely good for you and rich in vitamins. Why is it that the better something is for you the worse it seems to taste?

The meadow is full of life with butterflies aplenty including the likes of small blue, ringlet and meadow brown. Watch for lapwings, skylarks and meadow pipits and if you are passing late in the evening or early dawn you might catch a glimpse of tawny and short-eared owls often seen by the quiet traveller.

Just as this path rejoins the main path watch for a small area of grassland with cowslip and cranesbill putting on a show depending on the season. The main path takes you through an area of woodland where alder and willow dominate; this area is brilliant for our migrant warblers. We have willow warblers, garden warblers, blackcaps and chiffchaffs to delight your ears. And even if you cannot tell the difference between the species the sound is still a great pleasure. I love recording the birds at dawn especially in the spring along this path.

Further along the path you will come across a ramp on your right hand side that takes you over the railway bridge.

PRESTON ISLAND

This path is a circular route of approximately 2.7 miles (4.3 km) and is more exposed to the elements of the wind and sea. Proceed to the right and this path will take you on a horseshoe route to join the main path at the pedestrian railway bridge. The path is skirting the south side of the ash lagoons and is bordered with a sea wall on one side and areas of meadow and woods on the other. Look out for melilot and goosefoot growing along the side of the path. This path is great for all who love the song of skylarks. We have high numbers breeding in the meadows along with meadow and rock pipits. The sea wall eventually stops and is replaced by stone armour.

If you are into fossils then these large stones are like a treasure chest waiting to be explored. As you approach the crown of the horseshoe path watch and listen for our terns in late summer. It is a sound that always puts a smile on my face as it reminds me of summer holidays in a caravan next to the beach when I was a young lad.

If the tide is out then the rocks in front of you are Craigmore and the Dog Rock, and you should spend a minute to see what is using them. Both grey and common seals are often seen and at the right time of year, you can hear them making that strange barking noise at each other.

Just as you turn north on the far section of the horseshoe, there is a reed bed sewage works on your right, maybe not a nice thing, but it does have great environmental value.

We have breeding grasshopper warblers there and they sound exactly like grasshoppers, some people describe it as like a fishing reel sound.

Proceed onwards between the fence lines and Preston Island will open up in front of you. The site started off as an island in the Forth and has now been surrounded by reclaimed land.

Preston Island was 'Floating Bob's' pride and joy and I will leave you to discover who he was by reading the various information panels. The island is a splendid and now rare example of saltpans and coal workings on the east coast.

The island also used to be home to the salt and coal workers. Eventually, an illicit whisky distillery was run from there before being found out by the Excise man due to the 'wrang reek'. The information panels will explain all. This detour is well worth that little extra effort just for the cultural heritage of Preston Island alone.

Before we leave Preston Island cast an eye over to the east and there you will see an area of wetland with scattered willow. This area is good for sedges and breeding wading birds. In spring listen for snipe drumming in flight, a weird noise, but once recognised never forgotten. Teal and wigeon often roost here when the tide is high. Unfortunately this area tends to dry out in the summer and this hampers its potential.

Follow the path round and where the two fences border it, keep a look out, in spring, for the common spotted orchids in the path margins. The path will take you past an area of willow and alder on your right hand side. Look past this woodland and out onto the mudflat where the Bluther Burn runs past. Here you will get an appreciation of how deep the mud is if the tide is right. It's a lot deeper than your wellies as I found out to my dismay.

Follow the path around and past the lagoon entrance to meet up with the main path at the ramp on your left hand side that takes you over the railway bridge. Now you have walked this stretch I can reveal that this area you have just come through is where the elusive and some say mythical large cats have been sighted!

After crossing the railway bridge turn right and proceed along the path that will bring you out at the Scottish Power Ash Lagoons entrance. The next stretch will take you along pavements and you will pass on your left hand side the entrance to Valleyfield Woods – worth a visit due to its rich landscape history designed by Humphrey Repton for the Preston family.

As you pass through the mining village of Newmills you can replenish your food and drink if necessary all ready for the next stretch. The path ends at a small car park just past the rail bridge at Torryburn.

Did You Know?
Torry Bay Nature Reserve

Torry Bay is nothing if not unusual. In the heart of an area punctuated by modern industry lies a haven for wildlife. With views across the Forth to the industrial complex of Grangemouth, the shadow of Longannet Power Station nearby and vast Ash Lagoons at its centre, it may seem incongruous that this is an area designated as a nature reserve. Yet, Torry Bay was identified as a local nature reserve in 1996 with the aim of conserving and protecting the area. Not only that, the area is also part of a Site of Special Scientific Interest (SSSI), part of the Firth of Forth Special Protection Area (SPA) and a Ramsar site – a wetland of international importance designated under the Ramsar Convention.

This impressive array of titles is due to the significance of the intertidal mudflats at Torry Bay and the birdlife that they attract. Mudflats are commonly found in estuaries, particularly in the most sheltered areas and although mudflats are a relatively common sight round the British coastline, the example found at Torry Bay is held up as a particularly good example.

The deceptively barren appearance of mudflats disguises a wealth of activity and belies the value that this environment can provide. The sediment exposed at low tide is a rich mix of silt and clay – and an increasing proportion of sand in areas closer to the mouth of the estuary. This sediment is full of organic material and brimming with nutrients and invertebrates, making it an invaluable environment for a wide variety of species including migratory birds.

The role of mudflats in absorbing the energy from waves is also significant, as

The tide is out at Torry Bay Nature Reserve

is the fact that they are not usually used for recreational purposes: providing an important habitat that remains undisturbed by human activity throughout the year.

But, it's not just peace and tranquillity that draws birds to Torry Bay. One square metre of mud is said to contain a mind-boggling 60,000 laver spire snails and ragworms in their thousands, ensuring there is a never-ending supply of food for birds spending the winter on the shores of the Forth. Winter welcomes large numbers of great crested grebe, shelduck, wigeon, redshank, curlew and dunlin to the shore while ringed plover and greenshank are more likely to be spotted in the autumn. The careful management of the site at the nearby ash lagoons has led to increased planting of wildflower meadows – with the aim of having up to 20 different species within two square metres – that will make the area even more attractive to species such as meadow pipits and bees too.

Species in the area are carefully monitored by the local Coastal Path Ranger – aided by a team of volunteers – who carry out regular bird counts and inspections of the nesting sites for birds such as sand martins that nest in the area in great numbers. Although more rare species are occasionally spotted in the area, management of the nature reserve is largely done for the benefit of the majority, rather than the exception, to ensure that this area retains the qualities that attract such large volumes of birds.

But it's not just birds that enhance the attraction of this exceptional area. Plants such as melilot, common spotted orchid and eelgrass are just some of the plant life that can be seen on a visit to the area and orange tip butterflies are also common. With the familiar Fife Coastal Path waymarkers now in place along this stretch of the route – and long-term plans for bird hides throughout the reserve – this stretch of the coastal path has secured its future as a favourite for wildlife enthusiasts.

LONGANNET ASH LAGOONS

In an incongruous marriage between industry and environment, the Valleyfield Ash Lagoons on Fife's southern coastline provide a little understood solution to the age-old problem of industrial waste. To the untrained eye these vast, uncompromising lagoons look like something more likely to be found on the surface of the moon than in the east of Scotland, but the reality is almost as strange. For, right in the middle of a nature reserve – and a Site of Special Scientific Interest no less – ash from nearby Longannet Power Station is pumped into enormous holes in the ground and can provide real, tangible benefits to the local environment.

But to suggest that it's merely a case of pumping waste ash into holes in the ground is to overstate the simplicity of the project. This is a long-term feat of engineering, being undertaken here on a larger scale than anywhere else in Scotland.

The ash lagoons, of which the first was constructed in 1968, make use of land close to the shore line as well as reclaiming land from the Firth of Forth, so much so that Preston Island, once famed for salt panning, is no longer an island. The purpose of the lagoons – standing at approximately 25 hectares each – is to store and stabilise the ash from Longannet Power Station.

As anyone who has ever sat too close to a traditional coal fire well knows, the burning of coal produces a huge amount of dust and ash. And the volume produced at a site of Longannet's proportions is enormous. Measures put in place at the power station capture this dust and in a highly controlled process stop it from being released into the atmosphere.

The ash that is captured forms two main types: pulverised fuel ash and furnace bottom ash. It is the lighter of these two, the pulverised fuel ash, which is mixed with seawater and pumped along the coastline into the artificially constructed lagoons.

Steep embankments, also made of this pulverised ash, form a bund to hold the liquid ash securely and allow it to settle over time and the water to drain safely away, back into the Forth. But, as with most good solutions, there are conditions and compromises. Longannet's operators must ensure that their work at the Valleyfield Lagoons complies with the complex conditions of a Pollution Prevention Control Licence from SEPA as well as those of a Waste Management Licence.

To many making the leap from industrial waste to a site of national interest for wildlife and biodiversity seems incredible, but the ash lagoons are testament to what can be done when the needs of both industry and environment are met. Once the water has drained away from the lagoons and the settled ash is all that remains, the lagoons are capped using colliery shale. Left to their own devices native plant species will colonise this area within a year, providing both open ground and greenery for local bird life to use.

As the site is largely inaccessible to humans, the lure of undisturbed and safe territory draws a wide variety of birds, from skylarks to curlew and shelducks to wigeon. And with careful management of the site, the potential is vast. The planting of wildflower meadows on some areas of the lagoons can result in as many as 20 different plant species inhabiting an area of just two square metres and when seen on a much larger scale, it is easy to understand how this can provide much-needed habitats for wildlife such as bees, meadow pipits and butterflies.

Current plans allow for the lagoons to continue being in operation until 2030, by which time it is envisaged that the area will provide a vast array of habitats and diversity for plant and animal life, as well as facilities for observing them, such as bird hides.

These plans will ensure that what is the final part of an industrial process can be fully integrated into the environment and provide benefit to Torry Bay Local Nature Reserve.

LOCAL BUSINESSES

TORRYBURN

Food and Beverage

Torry Bay Hotel, 100 Main Street, Torryburn, KY12 8LS. Tel: 01383 882050

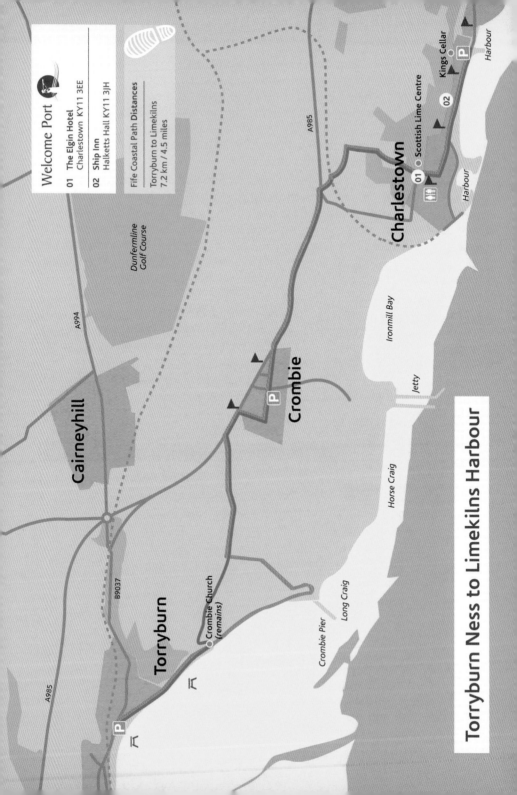

Torryburn Ness to Limekilns Harbour

Welcome Port

01 The Elgin Hotel
Charlestown KY11 3EE

02 Ship Inn
Halketts Hall KY11 3JH

Fife Coastal Path Distances

Torryburn to Limekilns
7.2 km / 4.5 miles

Dunfermline
Golf Course

Cairneyhill

Torryburn

Crombie

Crombie Church
(remains)

Crombie Pier

Long Craig

Horse Craig

Jetty

Ironmill Bay

Charlestown

01 ○ Scottish Lime Centre

Kings Cellar

02

Harbour

Harbour

Harbour

A994

A985

A985

B9037

CHAPTER THREE

TORRYBURN NESS TO LIMEKILNS HARBOUR

THIS section of the Fife Coastal Path is 4.5 miles long (7.2 km) and easy walking. It starts at Torryburn and follows the shore before cutting inland at the old Kirk, then skirting Crombie village before descending through quaint Charlestown to finishing at the historic harbour of Limekilns.

Start at the Ness Car Park right on the shore at Torryburn where you will find information panels on the Coastal Path and the nature reserve that covers the area of mudflats facing you. The locals refer to this area as 'Oor Muddy Beach.' Please take care and do not venture onto the mud, as the depth of the mud in certain areas is over a couple of metres.

The mudflats at this point are reckoned to be one of the widest of all the Forth estuary mudflats and the tide can race in. The richness of the mud gives the nature reserve an international importance and attracts a great variety of waders and ducks. In the winter months watch out and listen for the whistles of the wigeon – not all ducks go 'quack quack', as these ducks 'whistle' – but it is not a tune. I can do a fair impression of the call so look carefully if you hear them, as it might just be the rare bald-headed Ranger!

Proceed along the path to the right and this will take you on to Shore Road. As you walk along you will pass a few patches of rare saltmarsh communities. Probably the easiest area to find is to look out for three leaning, sitting stools on the right with an arch in the sea wall that the path crosses over with the Torry Burn beneath. Here you will find glasswort, sea plantain, sea aster, sea thrift and eelgrass all of which are a botanist's delight.

If the weather is bad or you fancy a bit of a woodland walk instead of continuing along the waterfront then pass through the doorway in the adjacent wall (watch out for some large holes to the side of the path) and follow the woodland path along. This area is known as The Craig – it has lots of mature beech trees and the ground is carpeted with ivy.

Notice how woodlands are always cooler in the summer and warmer in the winter than the surrounding areas. It's like they have their own special weather. The woodland path will rejoin the coastal path through a stone doorway. Have a look at the sculptured lintel. I cannot make out all the details and words due to erosion of the stone, however try to see what you can make out.

If you opted for the waterfront option then further along the Shore Road you will find a few benches and a couple of picnic tables, ideal to take out your Kincardine flask and watch for the crosses on St Bride's birds. Eventually the path crosses a bit of cobbled brick path with the sculptured lintel doorway to the woodland adjacent. Here you have a choice to take a detour to Crombie Point or to follow the main path that heads left.

MAIN PATH

Climb the steep incline passing the bridge abutments near the top to arrive at the gate of the old Kirk and graveyard. Unfortunately the old Kirk and graveyard are not open to the public due to some of the walls being derelict and dangerous. You now continue along the farm track, but just before you do look for a patch of common comfrey on your right. This was used years ago to stop bleeding and help mend broken bones, hence the local name of 'bone knit'.

The path is hedged with hawthorn and witch hazel and this is an excellent area to see tree sparrows that are sadly now an uncommon sight in our countryside. Also keep your ears peeled for yellowhammers whose song of 'a little bit of bread and no cheeeeeese' is usually heard from the telegraph wires overhead. The farm track eventually joins up with the road to Crombie Point.

CROMBIE POINT DETOUR

For this detour continue straight ahead along Shore Road past a large patch of purple teasel – a much-loved plant of bees and butterflies in the summer and seed provider for finches in the winter. I once saw a small flock of snow buntings here as they stopped off on their migration before crossing the North Sea.

Common comfrey - or the 'bone knit' plant

I never fail to be surprised as to what turns up on our shoreline. Just further along the beach I found a two-metre long sunfish and later that same week a fisherman at Alloa caught a large swordfish. The Forth is full of surprises for those who take the time to watch and wait.

As you continue on you will pass a beautiful house with a spooky name 'The Witches' Tower' and with its wrought iron gates it just adds to the eeriness. I wonder if there is a connection between the house and Torryburn Church where one former minister, a Rev. Allan Logan, was a self-appointed witch hunter and was responsible for the death by burning of some unfortunate locals.

Continuing on, you will find in the path margins plants such as tansy and cranesbill before eventually arriving at Crombie Point where the road turns up just at the Black Anchor – another spooky name for such a lovely building.

Before climbing up the hill, nip round the corner and you get a view of the old

This sunfish was an unusual find on the shoreline

derelict pier of Crombie Point. It is said that Jules Verne landed at the pier over 150 years ago. Many birds use the pier and often you will find large black, green and white eider ducks amongst them. They make that lovely deep cooing noise that again seems strange to me for a duck. Maybe it's a lullaby for us as we used to use their nesting down for bedding.

The road from Crombie Point climbs up steeply to pass Bullions Farm Cottages to rejoin the Coastal Path at the sharp corner junction with the farm track leading to the old Kirk.

The coastal path now continues mainly along roads as we avoid the Ministry of Defence establishment at Crombie. As you follow the narrow road you will pass a few sporadic mature trees of ash, beech and oak until the road joins with the main A985. I often wonder when passing mature trees what changes they have seen and what the future will hold for them. These trees were here long before I was born and hopefully will still be there long after I am gone. A little pondering thought on a walk is always a good thing.

At the junction with the main road, have a look north and you should see the transmitters on top of Knockhill – well known for its racing circuit. If you then look slightly right, the spires of Dunfermline can be seen.

Follow the road along until you arrive at the village of Crombie and turn right, up Farm Road, which goes around the outside of the village and past the car park. If the weather is good you can get some nice views over the arable land to Bo'ness across the water. At the junction, head along Orchard Grove and on to the path that will bring you safely back to the main A985 road.

The next section is all downhill along the cycle path off the busy main road through arable farmland. The farm on your right is Waukmill and the owner keeps a nice collection of farm implements that are well worth a look as you pass by. Watch out for the concealed entrance a little further on at Waukmill Farm Lodge. A little past the lodge we turn right then sharp left to head towards the Scottish Lime Centre and here we are back onto farm track which gets rougher as we head towards Charlestown.

The Scottish Lime Centre is a charity, which through training and practical experience promotes the traditional use of lime for the repair and conservation of much of our valuable building heritage. It's a very appropriate location for them as we find out as we continue our journey to Limekilns.

Follow the path round and up the slight incline until it starts to descend into a leafy plantation between Broomknowe and Rocks Plantation, with a stone wall on your right and the disused quarry on your left. I like to call this area Squirrel Alley, as I constantly see grey squirrels here. Watch for them eating the beech mast on both sides of the track. Look for a yellow sign saying 'Danger Disused Quarry' then look at the mature beech tree behind and above. This is a good spot to see the squirrels, but it's a pity they are not our native reds. The track continues on becoming Rocks Road as we enter Charlestown.

Charlestown was founded in 1761 by Charles Bruce, the 5th Earl of Elgin, to house the workmen for his lime works. As you head down Main Road you pass one of the prettiest sets of cottages on your right hand side, all surrounding the village green. I like the street names of these cottages – North Row, South Row, Cross Row, Hall Row and Double Row – all stating exactly what and where they are. Simple stuff. Look out for one of the original red telephone boxes complementing the red pantile roofs of many of the little cottages. Pantiles were imported as ballast for the ships returning from the Continent and are much a feature of the east coast of Fife as are crow step gables. These features will be seen throughout your journey on Fife's Coastal Path.

The road descends steeply and changes construction from tarmac into cobbles – in keeping with the historical flavour of the area. At the bottom of the hill you can take a short detour along Saltpans and pass the old harbour before coming to the actual limekilns themselves. This row of limekilns dates from the 18th century. Take a few minutes out and read the information panel and look for butterflies on the buddleia that grows unchecked throughout the site.

Return now to the bottom of the brae and progress along the wide promenade catching good views of the Forth Bridges – our final destination for my stretch of the Coastal Path.

The tide comes right up to the promenade wall and is a good viewpoint for terns passing by and also roosting on the rocks. Watch for my favourite, the sandwich tern. You will recognise them as they are the largest of our terns and in my opinion the noisiest, plus the only ones that have a yellow tip to an all-black beak. Stroll along the promenade until you arrive at the harbour – our destination for this stretch.

You can sit on one of the benches and listen for that classic 'keeric, keeric' call of my favourite terns and if you are lucky you can then watch these white sea swallows diving for fish, a true and simple pleasure. The rocks to the east are one of their favourite roosting places when season and tide are right.

Did You Know?
Lime Industry

In a tale of exploiting the Earth's natural assets to their fullest potential, the quiet western edge of Fife's coastline was once home to a thriving industry that dominated the market in Europe – that of lime production. At one time, the small villages of Limekilns and nearby Charlestown were producing lime in such high quantities it is estimated that almost one third of building lime used in the United Kingdom was coming from Fife – and it was also being exported across the world.

This part of the Fife coastline is rich in limestone, a natural substance largely made up of calcium carbonate and most commonly known as chalk. Once quarried out of the ground, the limestone is burnt at high temperatures to produce quicklime and then water is added in a skilled process, called slaking, to form the lime that forms the basis for a range of building materials.

A sandwich tern

Sometimes thought of as history's cement, lime has been used in the construction of buildings for thousands of years. In its simplest form, the slaked lime – lime putty – was used most commonly for internal plastering and lime wash. When aggregates, such as sand, are added the lime can be used for a whole range of building work, as its qualities such as strength and durability can be adapted to the conditions at hand.

Historically the use of additives such as horsehair was not uncommon, as it was known to strengthen the lime plaster against wear and tear. But lime produced in Fife wasn't just used in building construction. As many a gardener will testify the addition of lime to the soil can improve the prospects of many plants and it is said that the lime from Fife was used to support one of Scotland's other great industries – that of whisky production – through its use on fields of barley.

Limekilns Harbour

Whatever its final purpose however, it was clear by the 18th century that lime from Fife's western shores could not largely meet the demands of a changing Britain and although lime had been produced on a small scale at Limekilns for hundreds of years, it took the vision of Charles, the 5th Earl of Elgin to change the industry to one of vast proportions.

Charles was said to be visionary in his creation of Charlestown. But for some, this may have been seen as the ultimate egotistical project. Although industry was already established in the village on a very small scale in the form of an iron mill, he was keen to make the most of the natural assets of his estate and set about creating a village, which would provide the workers for his growing lime industry. Against the odds he did so, with the layout of his new village marking out the initials 'CE', as his formal title was Charles Elgin. However, in spite of this display of vanity, Charles also committed to creating an exemplary village and ensured that the village had facilities often unheard of at the time, including a school, a shop and a laundry.

The construction of a number of new kilns – bringing the total in the area to 20 – ensured the village was able to operate at full capacity and the reputation of Charlestown soon spread. A small railway provided transportation for the quarried lime to reach the kilns and the construction of a bigger and better harbour made the export of the lime products possible on a grand scale.

Much of the building work of Georgian Edinburgh is said to have used lime from Fife's quarries, perhaps as a result of the Earl's reputed friendship with fellow Fifer and famous neoclassical architect, Robert Adam, with a large part of

Edinburgh's much-admired New Town owing more than a passing nod across the Forth to Fife. Such was the success of Elgin's lime industry that production continued long after his death until well into the 20th century until the kilns closed in the mid 1950s. Those making their way along the Coastal Path can still view these vast kilns and explore the historical village of Charlestown itself, now a world away from the bustling, hot industry that once dominated its streets.

The kilns themselves now fall under the care of the National Trust and the Scottish Lime Centre, based in Charlestown who are working to ensure the traditional skills are preserved for future generations.

LOCAL BUSINESSES

CHARLESTOWN

Accommodation

The Elgin Hotel and Restaurant,
Charlestown, KY11 3EE.
Tel: 01383 872257
www.theelginhotel.com
(Welcome Port)

Post Office

The Sultry and Post Office, 14 Rocks Road, KY11 3EN. Tel: 01383 872249

LIMEKILNS

Accommodation

Il Pescatore, Hotel and Restaurant,
40 Main Street, Limekilns, KY11 3HL.
Tel: 01383 872999

Food and Beverage

The Ship Inn, Halketts Hall, Limekilns, KY11 3HJ.
Tel: 01383 872247 (Welcome Port)

Bruce Arms, 2 Main Street, Limekilns, KY11 3HL. Tel: 01383 872259

Post Office

Limekilns Post Office, 28 Main Street, KY11 3HL. Tel: 01383 872279

Limekilns Harbour to North Queensferry

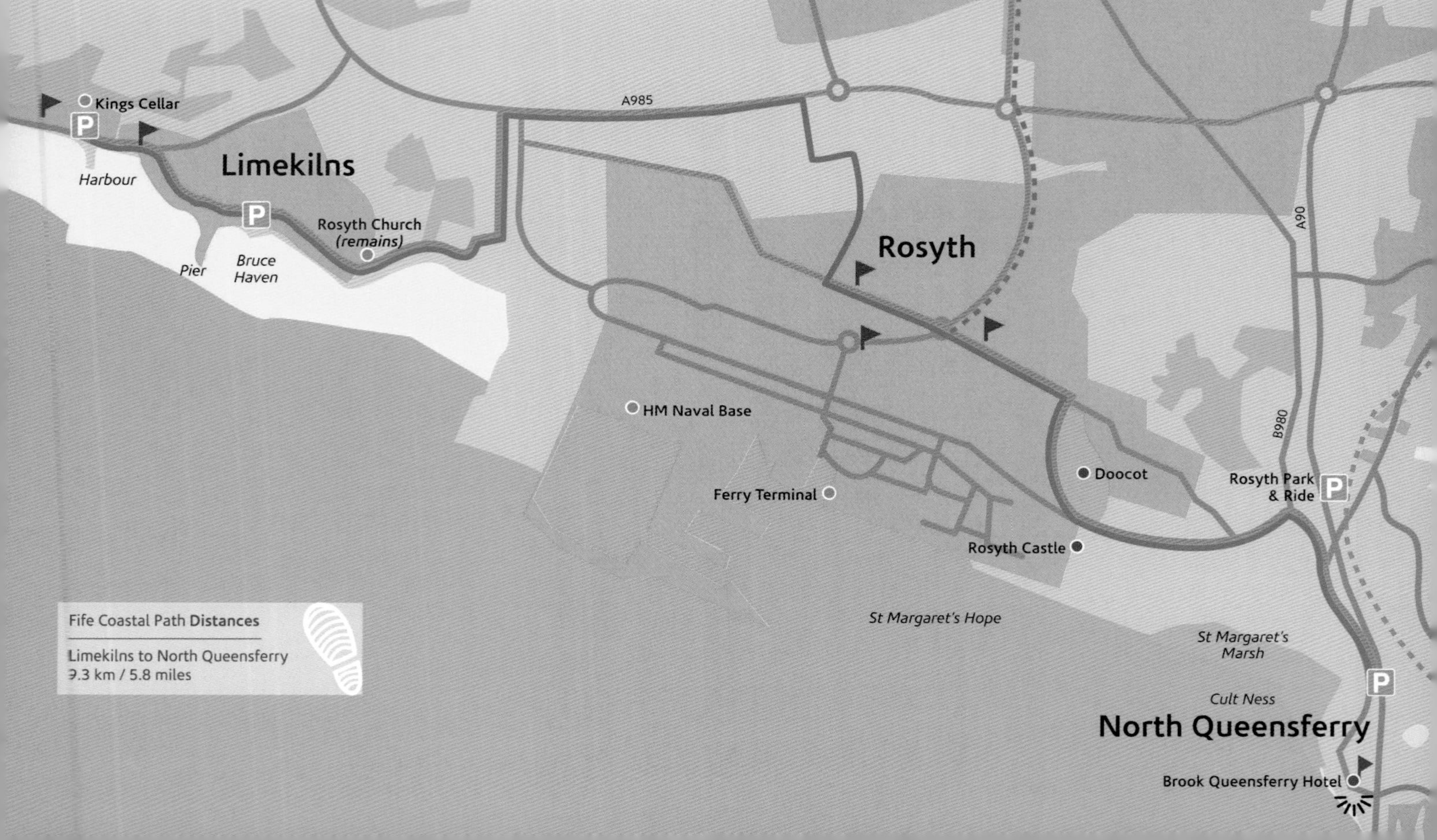

A90

B980

A985

North Queensferry

Brook Queensferry Hotel

Cult Ness

St Margaret's Marsh

St Margaret's Hope

Rosyth Park & Ride

Doocot

Rosyth

Rosyth Castle

Ferry Terminal

HM Naval Base

Limekilns

Rosyth Church (remains)

Bruce Haven

Pier

Kings Cellar

Harbour

Fife Coastal Path Distances

Limekilns to North Queensferry
9.3 km / 5.8 miles

CHAPTER FOUR

LIMEKILNS HARBOUR TO NORTH QUEENSFERRY

THIS section of the Fife Coastal Path is 5.8 miles long (9.3 km) and easy walking. It starts at the harbour and follows the coast past historic Rosyth Church and up to Brucehaven. From here onwards you are on roadside pavements as you skirt Rosyth Naval Base before descending into North Queensferry.

You are now on the final and longest section of my stretch of the Coastal Path and here it starts at the picturesque harbour of Limekilns. Limekilns is believed to be older than neighbouring Charlestown and can date its history back to the 14th century. Please spend a minute or two to sit on the benches and view the panorama. The harbour often has a flotilla of small yachts and you should see your destination, the Forth Bridges, in the background.

Leave the harbour behind and turn right to walk along the wide promenade and watch for black-headed gulls along the sea wall. Hopefully they will let you get close enough to notice that their heads are a chocolate colour and not black after all. If the tide is out then the next couple of bays are excellent for watching waders. If you are a keen birdwatcher, look out for rare all-white gulls in the winter months with both Iceland and glaucous gulls having been sighted here.

At the end of the promenade turn right along Red Row, bordered by a small patch of sandy beach. Anyone fancy a paddle? Give it a miss in the winter though! At the end of Red Row you should see another pier in front of you and a small bay adjacent. The area to the right is pretty good for having a 'guddle about' in the small rock pools. However watch your step on the seaweed, as it can be pretty slippery at times.

The road turns up to the left to join Brucehaven Road and you just continue along past the Scout Hall and Forth Cruising Club. Look for a gate leading to a little lane with a stone wall on your left and follow this along. The area then opens up into a nice little sandy bay where the cruising club often have a few yachts and dinghies berthed, making it all very picturesque. This area is known as Brucehaven Harbour – however many of the locals still refer to it by its older name of Capernaum.

I wonder if there is any link between its old name and the fishing village of Capernaum that is mentioned in the Bible. Watch for the buddleia and tansy that skirt the wall, which is often a good place to see our butterflies. Nothing says summertime to me as much as a picture of buddleia in full bloom covered in small tortoiseshells and peacock butterflies. I could even forgive the buddleia for being a non-native plant.

This little path is joined on the left by Windylaw Path, a pretty name that hides

The history of Rosyth Church goes back to the 12th century

a creepy past. I will let you discover the reason why when you get there. You are now faced with a choice either to continue along the official route, or to take a little detour up Windylaw Path. I will describe each and you can then choose which you fancy.

MAIN COASTAL PATH

The path continues along and round the corner to arrive at Rosyth Church where there is a bench just at the entrance if you want to sit and take in the view. The church itself is worth exploring with its old graves and it can trace its history back to the 12th century.

I like the feel of this graveyard, very tranquil with its proximity close to the shore. However, this proximity gave it problems during the grave-robbing era, as it was remote from dwellings and just across the water from the main market for bodies at the time – namely the medical college of Edinburgh.

The seawall in front of the bench often has a cascade of mayweed in the summer months. Good views of the Rosyth Dockyard with the bridges behind can be seen at this point. The path has a sharp pull-up where ruderal plus fern habitats border the path with arable fields adjacent.

On a good day if you look south you can glimpse Hopetoun House peeping through the trees across the water. Now for all who enjoy a festive tipple, the bushes along this stretch are blackthorn, which gives us sloes for gin. Please remember only pick if you are confident in your plant identification and only take what you need.

The route now skirts Windylaw Edge woodland that is dominated by tall poplar trees. Follow the path and just after one of the sharp bends a gap appears in the bushes. If it is spring and early morning or dusk, nip into this woodland (rough dirt path) and listen for our leaf warblers. It is worth getting up early just to go there. I heard a brilliant dawn chorus in that little wood, loads of warblers, robins, dunnock and whitethroat. The dirt track rejoins the path in a couple of hundred yards. If you decide to stick to the main path it goes round a few sharp corners then has a really steep long incline up to Brucehaven and the A985.

WINDYLAW DETOUR

Follow the path up past the houses until you come to a signpost for Pattiesmuir, where you will then skirt the perimeter of fields as you head up to the mature woodland at Windylaw Head. This lovely mature and open woodland made up of mainly beech, oak and sycamore trees allows for a pleasant shaded stroll that rejoins the Coastal Path a few hundred yards south of Brucehaven.

Where the path meets the A985 turn right and head alongside the road. The next stretch is through the town of Rosyth as we avoid the Naval Dockyard. After about 1.2km you will turn off from the A985 and head down a dogleg path. This is another good place to collect sloe berries for your gin. Follow this path until it joins Brankholm Lane. Keep an eye on the playing fields on your left as they often have roosting gulls and on occasions, a few waders.

The next section of the path is through the housing scheme and across the main roads generally in an easterly direction. However it can be confusing so watch for signs on lampposts etc. The route goes from Brankholm Lane into Wilson Way then down to the junction with Hilton Road, then across the main road and onto Ferry Toll Road. Follow the road for approximately 250 metres where you then go through a pair of metal gates on your right hand side.

The path then heads down the brae past the Heritage trail which is worth a wee detour, as it is a short pleasant circular walk through mature woodland approximately half a kilometre long.

Leave the path where the information panel is and step into the wood where you will find the 'Doocot'. I like this building that has 1500 square apertures inside for the pigeons to nest in. I am not sure I would like to work in it though – 1500 pigeons create a lot of guano! Have a look at the lintel over the door to the rear of the building – you can still make out the carved serpent. I believe this is a depiction of the old Bible saying of 'Be ye wise as serpents and harmless as doves'.

Considering the amount of guano I am not so sure of the harmless doves bit.

The whole building has a feel of bats about it. I have never checked if there is a colony there, but I bet there is. I will put this down on my things to do list.

Back on the path, follow it down until you arrive at the junction with Milne Road. Looking across the road to the south you will see Rosyth Castle which dates back to the early 15th century. It is worth a walk across to get a good view of the Castle, which reputably had historic links to Cromwell, Mary Queen of Scots and St Margaret, wife of King Malcolm Canmore. Unfortunately, there is no information panel. You can read more about the Castle at the end of this chapter.

The Coastal Path follows along the main road, but before you reach the roundabout you will be approaching where the new bridge is going to be built and there has been a lot of discussion on what the bridge should be called.

I fancy something like 'Wisna Cheap Bridge', or maybe the 'Fifth Bridge', however they will probably call it something sensible like 'Kingdom Bridge'. It would be nice to view it, let your mind wander and come up with your own name.

My wife and I have done a few long distance walks and we often used to change place names. It's amazing how often the name sticks in your mind. A fine example would be Conic Hill, near Balmaha on the West Highland Way. We changed it to 'Cuddle Ma Hump' and we still remember its name as that, although it was many years ago we climbed it.

St Margaret's Marsh is off to the right and is an area of reed bed worth a visit

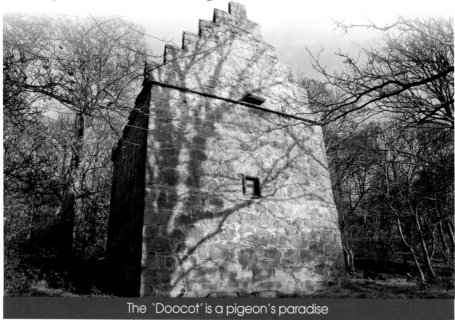

The 'Doocot' is a pigeon's paradise

for its variety of bird life. A few rare species turn up here in this Site of Special Scientific Interest (SSSI) but telling you what you may see will spoil the fun and anticipation of the discovery. Look for birds both small and large. Happy hunting!

Follow the road as it leads you into North Queensferry. If you have time and a head for heights I would recommend walking across the Forth Road Bridge. The views are great to the west – 'there's that chimney again' – and it's amazing how you can feel the bridge move. I love looking down onto the seabirds flying underneath and if you are lucky, some of our more unusual terns may be seen. To the east is the vast shoreline of the Kingdom of Fife all for you to explore.

As you come into North Queensferry there is a little area of mudflat between the bridges and it often holds a few waders such as oystercatchers, redshanks and sometimes godwits, but only if you time it right and the tide is out. Then comes a favourite view of mine. You have to be standing under the Road Bridge looking south through all the arch abutments. You will see when you get there.

Sadly we are coming to the end of my section with the entrance to the next section up on the left at the junction between The Brae and Old Kirk Road. I hope you have enjoyed the western part of the Coastal Path and I wish you 'Bon Voyage' and 'Haste Ye Back' as I pass you into the capable hands of my fellow Ranger, Stewart Bonar.

Did You Know?
Rosyth Castle

In a town now best known for a century of naval history and its thriving docks, the last thing you'd expect to find might be a castle. Yet, Rosyth Castle lies on the edges of the Naval Dockyard. This 15th century castle is every bit as interesting as its location is surprising. Just a short distance from Orchardhead Wood, near Livesay Road at the eastern side of the Europarc complex, the remains of the castle and the adjacent dovecot are slightly off the beaten track, and not well signposted, but certainly worth a look.

Rosyth Castle dates from around 1450 and although it is now well and truly part of the mainland, it originally stood on an outcrop and was only accessible when the tide was out – giving its occupants some added natural security during notoriously transient and troubled times. Even at the start of the 20th century the castle remained remote from the mainland: demonstrating just how much of the coastline has been reclaimed over the past century.

The original occupant of Rosyth Castle was Sir David Stewart, of the well-known Stewart or Steward dynasty, who held the Barony of Rosyth from the early 15th century until the start of the 18th century when it came into the hands of the Earl of Rosebery and thereafter the Earl of Hopetoun – better known for

Rosyth Castle dates from around 1450

the spectacular Hopetoun House and estate, directly across the Forth at South Queensferry. The Stewart family were descended from prominent Scottish figures – including Robert the Bruce – and the Rosyth Stewarts were also said to be distantly related to Mary Queen of Scots, and to the mother of Oliver Cromwell, Elizabeth Stewart.

The castle was initially constructed as a tower house, said by some to resemble a Norman fort, and marked by the enormously thick walls associated with the times. The three-storey dwelling was extended through the centuries to the shape now marked out by its remains, that of an L-shaped building which included a courtyard and features such as a vaulted ground floor.

Although the exact layout and purpose of all of the buildings within the grounds of the castle are, in places, hard to determine it is thought that at one time it would have served to accommodate servant's quarters, a chapel and a hall, as well as the living accommodation one might expect in a castle from this period. It is thought that as the castle fell to ruin after its occupancy, many parts of its stone work were removed, to be used elsewhere, leaving much of the castle stripped away almost to its foundations.

However, as with many historic buildings, when parts are changed throughout the centuries, those making the changes are keen to assert their authority and make their own mark on the building and, in the parts of the castle which still stand, this makes some features easier to date from the inscriptions they acquired at the time of their completion. The initials of James Stewart can be found in some stonework as can the inscription MR (representing Mary Queen of Scots) and the date 1561. Sadly, although Mary Queen of Scots' visits to nearby Dunfermline and its Abbey are well documented there are no records to indicate that she ever stayed in Rosyth Castle.

What is better documented however is the occupation of the castle in 1651 by Oliver Cromwell's forces during his Scottish campaign. Having heavily defeated the troops of David Leslie at Dunbar, Oliver Cromwell soon recognised that control of the Forth and the key area of Fife was crucial to a successful campaign in Scotland: giving access to the Scottish heartlands, and a firm footing for progression northwards.

The decisive battle took place at Inverkeithing on July 16 and 17, 1651, and records put the number of troops involved in the region of 10,000. The battle spread as far and wide as Pitreavie Castle in Dunfermline, and the island of Inchgarvie in the Forth also played a role. The Scots, however, suffered substantial losses, with some 2,000 lives being lost and a further 1,500 taken prisoner. Following his victory, a turning point in Cromwell's bid for control over the Scots, Cromwell's forces occupied Rosyth Castle before continuing their journey across Fife, towards the key battlegrounds at Stirling.

Surprisingly, despite its role in some of the most dramatic parts of Fife's history, Rosyth Castle remains little known – even to many locals. Its low-key location and even lower profile has secured its status as one of the county's best-kept secrets, but one deserving of another look nonetheless.

LOCAL BUSINESSES

NORTH QUEENSFERRY

Accommodation

St. Mungo's B&B, LowNorthcraig B&B, Battery Road, North Queensferry, KY11 1JZ. Tel: 01383 412299, www.northcraig-cottage.co.uk

Northcliff Self Catering Cottage, Main Street, North Queensferry, KY11 1HB. Tel: 01383 510666, www.northcliff.co.uk

The Queensferry Hotel, St. Margaret's Head, North Queensferry, KY11 1HP. Tel: 0800 435 165, www.brook-hotels.co.uk

The Albert Hotel, 25 Main Street, North Queensferry, KY11 1JG, www.the-albert-hotel.co.uk

Food and Beverage

The Wee Restaurant, Chapel Place, North Queensferry, KY11 1JT. Tel: 01383 616263 www.theweerestaurant.co.uk

Tourist Attraction

Deep Sea World, Forthside Terrace, North Queensferry, KY11 1JR. Tel: 01383 411880 www.deepseaworld.com

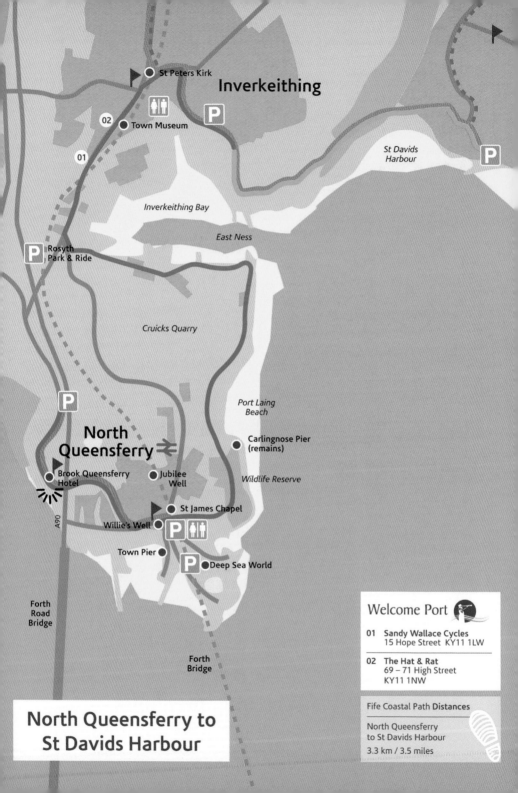

St Peters Kirk

Inverkeithing

02 Town Museum

01

Inverkeithing Bay

East Ness

St Davids
Harbour

Rosyth
Park & Ride

Cruicks Quarry

*Port Laing
Beach*

**North
Queensferry**

Carlingnose Pier
(remains)

Brook Queensferry
Hotel

Jubilee
Well

Wildlife Reserve

St James Chapel

Willie's Well

A90

Town Pier

Deep Sea World

Forth
Road
Bridge

Forth
Bridge

Welcome Port

01 Sandy Wallace Cycles
15 Hope Street KY11 1LW

02 The Hat & Rat
69 – 71 High Street
KY11 1NW

Fife Coastal Path **Distances**

North Queensferry
to St Davids Harbour

3.3 km / 3.5 miles

North Queensferry to
St Davids Harbour

CHAPTER FIVE

NORTH QUEENSFERRY TO ST DAVID'S HARBOUR

THE countryside has been a lifelong interest of mine, but 20 years ago I turned that interest into a profession by becoming a Countryside Ranger. I wanted to do something positive to conserve the countryside for the wildlife that depends on it for survival and to help people access and appreciate the value of these sites.

My favourite part of my patch is the walk from Kinghorn to Seafield, Kirkcaldy. It is a Site of Special Scientific Interest (SSSI) and has something for everybody. It has important geological features, including many fossils; architectural heritage at Seafield Tower; seals hauling on the rocks just offshore; winter wildfowl and waders are easily visible; and in the summer, many rare plants grow beside the path.

Countryside Ranger
Stewart Bonar

This section of the Fife Coastal Path begins at the car park in Battery Road, is 3.75 miles long (5.9 km) and easy walking. It takes in historic towns, industrial heritage and much of botanical and ornithological interest.

North Queensferry is named after Queen Margaret, wife of King Malcolm who reigned in the 11th century. It is said that Queen Margaret frequently used this area as a crossing point to travel between Dunfermline and Edinburgh. Our journey starts a little inland from the Forth, in front of the colourful Waterloo Well (shaped like Napoleon's hat) situated on the path at the bottom of the street called The Brae. The well was built to commemorate Wellington's epic and decisive victory over Napoleon at the Battle of Waterloo in 1815.

When we first opened the Path, local schoolchildren were asked to model something in clay that they might see on a journey along the path. The results can be seen in the plaques set into the wall beside the path. I particularly like those ones where you can see the actual fingerprints of the children who made them.

The path follows the old road up to the disused quarries of Carlingnose – the witch's nose – look on the map and you'll see it. This site has now developed a rich flora with many plants growing here that are uncommon in Fife such as bloody cranesbill, field gentian, burnet saxifrage, as well as a Scottish rarity, dropwort. For this reason the site is now a Scottish Wildlife Trust Nature Reserve and I am on the management committee for the site.

Just after you enter the Carlingnose Wildlife Reserve the area widens out and the path goes beside a rocky knoll, covered in grasses and wildflowers. When I first got involved in Carlingnose, this area was covered in gorse and hawthorn and the grassland had been crowded out. Since the grassland is the rarest habitat on the site, we took the decision to try to restore it. There were a lot of sceptical voices at the time, but every year since then, the wildflowers have thrived and I find it very rewarding to see the large spread of magenta-coloured bloody cranesbill compared to the small patch that was there before we began the work.

The site also offers tremendous views up the Forth. Behind are the famous rail and road bridges; while on the south shore there is the Hound Point tanker terminal

Dropwort - rarely seen in Scotland

with Cramond Island and Edinburgh further east. Three islands are visible – Inchmichery to the east, with Inchkeith in the distance and Inchcolm with its Abbey tucked in next to the shore beyond Dalgety Bay.

The path drops down now to where the area from the railway to the old pier used to make landfall. There is only a remnant of the pier remaining, an odd thing to have on a nature reserve. We decided to use it as an asset by trying to attract terns to nest on it. They like to nest on gravel so we had to put some down. We also used old car tyres as nest boxes to protect the young terns from gull attacks. This had been used successfully elsewhere, so we were quite confident that it would work.

I am not a great sailor at the best of times, so the prospect of bobbing about in a wee boat filled with gravel and car tyres did not appeal. Still it was all worthwhile and anything for the birds. Needless to say, after all our efforts and a couple of years on not a single tern had come near. Talk about ungrateful!

Then, one day, all the tyres disappeared after a storm and we thought it was such a wasted effort. But the storm and disappearance of the tyres was a blessing in disguise. As soon as the tyres disappeared, the terns started nesting. If you are there in summer, you should be able to see the adults plunge-diving for fish to carry back to the pier and feed their young.

The path drops down, then goes round into a hidden bay with a small stretch of beach before going through woodland towards the only active quarry left on

The Mercat Cross, in Inverkeithing

the peninsula. As you approach Cruicks Quarry, look over into Inverkeithing Bay where in winter, divers, grebes and goldeneye all congregate. Wading birds can also be seen probing into the mud for food. Redshank, oystercatcher, knot, dunlin and occasional ruff all use the bay in winter. I love the fact that so much wildlife can live quite happily alongside the industrial landscape of the bay. Beyond the Quarry, where quartz dolerite (whinstone) is still extracted, lies Jamestown Pond, an important site for amphibians, dragonflies and plants.

Going through Inverkeithing with its historic buildings and Mercat Cross, the path returns to the north side of the Bay near Inverkeithing Harbour where, up until 1867, the Halbeath Waggon Way used to bring coal from Dunfermline to be loaded onto ships. The path then hugs the coast for next mile or so. Growing by the path there is another uncommon Fife plant, sand leek.

Finally, the path reaches the outskirts of Dalgety Bay at St David's Harbour, so called because the south pier is built on a rock called St David's Castle. The harbour was built to export coal from Fordell, but is now part of a very modern development. Common seals may be seen on the rocks here, as well as many of the outcrops from here to Aberdour.

Did You Know?
The Forth Bridges

Whether you think of it as one of the new wonders of the world, a shining example of modern engineering, or just a welcome sight that means you're nearly home in Fife, there's no doubt that the Forth Rail Bridge is one of the most iconic images of modern Scotland. This vital link between Fife and the Lothians is just as crucial now for the many commuters who travel across it daily, as it was for those who welcomed its opening more than a century ago.

The Forth Bridge opened in March 1890 and remains the second longest cantilever bridge in the world, having lost first place to the Quebec Bridge in 1917. Designed by Englishmen Sir John Fowler and Sir Benjamin Baker – following the dismissal of Thomas Bouch at the helm – careful preparations were made for the construction of the bridge, with many lessons having been learnt from the Tay Bridge disaster, including the need to understand the impact the weather could have on the structure itself.

Once construction got underway more than 4,000 workers were involved but the building of the bridge cost the lives of almost 100 men, with many more being seriously injured throughout the seven-year process. A memorial to those who lost their lives was unveiled in 2007 and can be seen in South Queensferry on the south side of the bridge.

The formidable steel construction is 1.5 miles long and consists of three double cantilevers, with two main spans of just over 1,700 feet, side spans of 680 feet

The world-famous Forth Rail Bridge

and 15 smaller approach spans. The construction of the foundations alone is remarkable.

Each of the three main towers are supported by four separate granite foundations, each of which is held within iron caissons of 70 feet in diameter and sunk to a depth of 90 feet. In total it is estimated that almost 70,000 tonnes of steel and an incredible 6.5 million rivets were used in the construction. The last rivet, which was gold plated, was put in place by the Prince of Wales at the opening ceremony on the 4th March, 1890 and marked the beginning of a new era of travel across the Forth.

The bridge now sees the passage of up to 200 trains every day with limits placed on the speed and weight of trains, both for reasons of safety and to preserve the integrity of the bridge. And, the maintenance of the bridge is almost as big a feat as the construction itself with an extensive maintenance programme costing in the region of £40 million getting underway in the late 1990s.

This covered everything from steelwork to better lighting; not to mention the infamous painting of the bridge. The paint for the Forth Bridge was originally manufactured by Fife firm, Craig and Rose and the daunting task of painting the surface, estimated at 400,000 square metres, was said to be a never-ending process, giving rise to the much loved idiom 'It's like painting the Forth Bridge'. And while it's said to be a myth that the bridge was ever painted in such a way, it's a subject that continues to fascinate.

Painting finally came to an end in December 2011 after a decade of labour involving 200 workers. Advancing technology has seen the design and application of a new type of paint which will withstand all the elements and protect the bridge for at least 25 years, marking the end of an era – and a cliché lost for a whole new generation. But while the painting might come to an end, the iconic status of the bridge lives on. Scotland's largest listed structure has featured as the backdrop to a number of films, most notably The 39 Steps, and made its way into the Royal Mint by way of a one-pound coin in 2004.

The vital link that the Forth bridges provide between Fife and Edinburgh has never been in doubt, but this has been highlighted over recent years amid growing concern over the longevity of the road bridge.

The spectacular suspension bridge, which is over 1.5 miles long, has seen an unprecedented increase in the volume of traffic crossing it on a daily basis since it opened in 1964 and, more recently, concerns have grown over the impact of the weather on the structure. This has led to the commissioning of a new bridge, which is set to open in 2016. The new bridge will be designated as motorway and has been designed to hold two lanes and a hard shoulder in both directions, ensuring that this major artery will keep traffic moving across the Forth for years to come.

For more information on the development of the new Forth Crossing visit http://www.transportscotland.gov.uk/road/projects/forth-replacement-crossing.

The Waterloo Well - celebrating Wellington's famous victory against Napoleon

LOCAL BUSINESSES

INVERKEITHING

Accommodation

The Roods B&B, 16 Bannerman Avenue, Inverkeithing, KY11 1NG. Tel: 01383 415049, www.the-roods.co.uk

Boreland Lodge Hotel, 33-33 Boreland Road, Inverkeithing, KY11 1DA. Tel: 01383 413792, www.borelandlodgehotel.co.uk

Inglewood Guest House, 42, Boreland Road, Inverkeithing, KY11 1DA. Tel: 01383 410899, www.visitinglewood.co.uk

Food and Beverage

Maurizio's Takeaway, 60 High Street, Inverkeithing, KY11 1NN. Tel: 01383 412151

Cadora Chip Shop, 2 Townhall Street, Inverkeithing, KY11 1LX. Tel: 01383 413905

Happy Palace Takeaway, 10 High Street, Inverkeithing, KY11 1NN. Tel: 01383 417264

Maries Chinese Takeaway, 40 High Street, Inverkeithing, KY11 1NN. Tel: 01383 418055

Papa Joes Takeaway, 46 High Street, Inverkeithing, KY11 1NN Tel: 01383 411407

HSM Newsagents, 7-9 Church Street, Inverkeithing, KY11 1LG Tel: 01383 412670

Key Store, 57-59High Street, Inverkeithing, KY11 1NL

The Hat and Rat Pub, 69-71 High Street, Inverkeithing, KY11 1LW Tel: 01383 415613

The Queens Hotel, 8-10 Church Street, Inverkeithing, KY11 1LJ. Tel: 01383 413075 www.queenshotelinverkeithing.co.uk

The Spar Convenience Store, 45 High Street, Inverkeithing, KY11 1NL. Tel: 01383 419579

The Burgh Arms Pub, 22 High Street, Inverkeithing, KY11 1NN. Tel: 01383 413182

The Central Bar, 7-9 High Street, Inverkeithing, KY11 1NL. Tel: 01383 412096

The Half Crown Bar, 36 High Street, Inverkeithing, KY11 1NN. Tel: 01383 413350

Gallaghers Bar, 4 Heriot Street, Inverkiething, KY11 1ND. Tel: 01383 417247

Greggs Bakery, 47 High Street, Inverkeithing, KY11 1NL. Tel: 01383 412640

Baynes Bakery, 79 High Street, Inverkeithing, KY11 1NW. Tel: 01383 412386

Stephens the Bakers, 95 High Street, Inverkeithing, KY11 1NN. Tel: 01383 412681

Banks

ATM, High Street, Inverkeithing, KY11 1NL

Medical

Lindsay & Gilmour Pharmacy, 51High Street, Inverkeithing, KY11 1NL. Tel: 01383 412326

Co-op Pharmacy, 29 High Street, Inverkeithing, KY11 1NL Tel: 01383 412582

Outdoor

Sandy Wallace Cycles, 15 Hope Street, Inverkeithing, KY11 1LW. Tel: 01383 412915 www.swc.co.uk

Akela's Den, 27 Townhall Street, Inverkeithing, KY11 1LX Tel: 01383 428933 www.akelasden.co.uk

St Davids Harbour to Burntisland

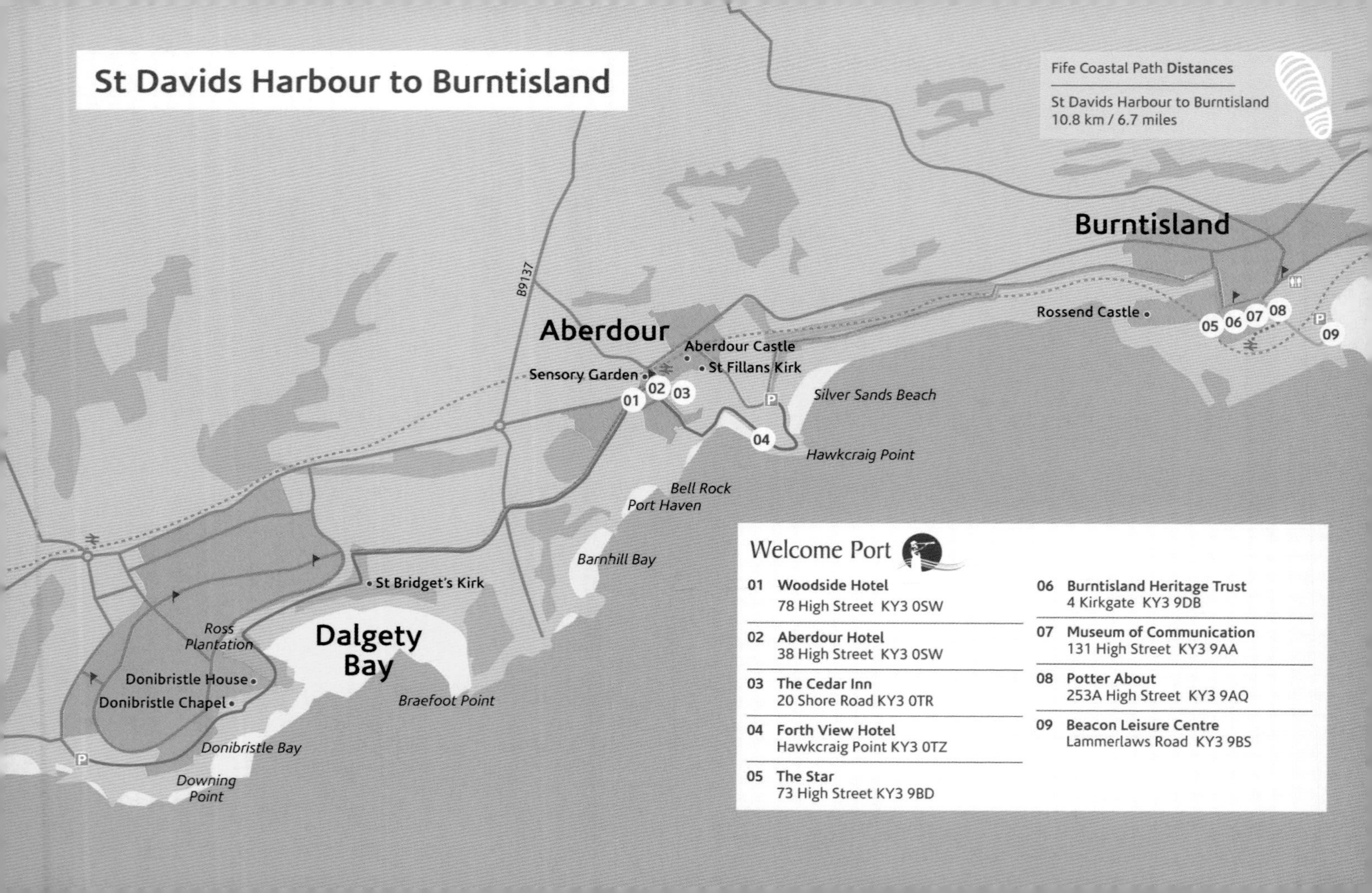

Fife Coastal Path Distances

St Davids Harbour to Burntisland
10.8 km / 6.7 miles

Welcome Port

01 **Woodside Hotel**
78 High Street KY3 0SW

02 **Aberdour Hotel**
38 High Street KY3 0SW

03 **The Cedar Inn**
20 Shore Road KY3 0TR

04 **Forth View Hotel**
Hawkcraig Point KY3 0TZ

05 **The Star**
73 High Street KY3 9BD

06 **Burntisland Heritage Trust**
4 Kirkgate KY3 9DB

07 **Museum of Communication**
131 High Street KY3 9AA

08 **Potter About**
253A High Street KY3 9AQ

09 **Beacon Leisure Centre**
Lammerlaws Road KY3 9BS

Burntisland

Rossend Castle

Aberdour

Aberdour Castle
St Fillans Kirk
Sensory Garden

Silver Sands Beach

Hawkcraig Point

Bell Rock
Port Haven

Barnhill Bay

St Bridget's Kirk

B9137

Dalgety Bay

Braefoot Point

Ross Plantation

Donibristle House
Donibristle Chapel

Donibristle Bay

Downing Point

CHAPTER SIX

ST DAVID'S HARBOUR TO BURNTISLAND

THIS section of the Fife Coastal Path is 7.5 miles long (12.2 km) and takes in the new town of Dalgety Bay, historic castles and churches, the famous beach at Aberdour and on through woodland to Burntisland.

Leaving St David's Harbour, the path goes through some small coastal woodlands and leads to Downing Point. This was the site of some WWI gun emplacements but also has some botanical interest with crow garlic, hare's-foot clover and Scots lovage all present.

Beyond the Point, make a small detour to visit the 18th century Donibristle Chapel, which contains the burial vault of the Earls of Moray. The Morays owned most of the land here for many centuries. All that remains of Donibristle House, the grand home of the Morays, is the servants' quarters and the old stable block, now both converted to flats. The developer has rebuilt the actual house in a similar style to the original and it gives an idea of how the mansion would have looked in its heyday.

It is hard to imagine it now, but Dalgety Bay was originally a fishing village. It became the site for a new town in the 1960s. The bay itself is an excellent site for wildfowl and waders during the winter, with shelduck, dunlin, knot and bar-tailed godwit all easily viewed. During the summer, terns can be seen plunge diving for fish in the bay.

The ruin of St Bridget's Kirk is a great spot to stop and have a look around. It dates from at least 1178 and is the only remaining part of the ancient village of Dalgety. The Kirk was consecrated in 1244 and was the burial ground for the Earls of Dunfermline. If you have time, then take a moment to sit and watch out over the Forth. It is a lovely quiet spot to enjoy the views, providing, that is, you don't find graveyards creepy.

After the Kirk, the path turns inland

Donibristle Chapel contains the burial vault of the Earls of Moray

The picturesque Silver Sands Bay - an excellent bathing beach

but will give superb views of Braefoot Bay Tanker Terminal where ethylene is exported. As you come out of the underpass, St Colme House is on the right where the ground is carpeted by snowdrops early in the year. I always love it when the snowdrops show because it is the first sign of new life in the year, even though spring itself may be some time away yet.

The track follows the north side of Aberdour Golf Course and offers good views offshore to Inchcolm, with its 12th century Abbey, before going through the village itself. Worthwhile detours here are to Aberdour Castle, which originated in the 12th century, although, most of what still stands dates from the 14th century and the 12th century St Fillan's Church. The path returns to the coast at Aberdour Harbour and leads on to Silver Sands Bay – an excellent bathing beach with modern facilities.

The next section towards Burntisland is mainly through old woodland, interesting both for the botanist and bird watcher. Note especially the falls of the Starley Burn just behind the castellated bridge. This burn is rich in lime that coats anything that falls into it, giving the falls their characteristic look. Every few years we have to chip away at the newly created limestone to make sure there is still room for the water to go under the bridge.

In Yorkshire, tourists often place objects into lime rich waterfalls and then come back later to collect the object, newly turned into stone. It is common to see all sorts of strange objects hanging in the water!

As the path opens out again you can look over the wall to Carron Harbour where limestone was shipped to the Carron Iron Works, in Falkirk. Between the harbour and Burntisland is a bay where it is common to see seals playing, or basking on rocks. The path now runs alongside a modern housing estate and then down to the High Street and on to the Beacon Leisure Centre.

Did You Know?
Islands in the Forth

If you've ever crossed the Forth Bridge on a sunny day, chances are you've looked down at the islands of the Forth and been intrigued by their sight – some rocky, some covered in birds, and one or two with oddly shaped buildings. And, a walk along the more westerly stretches of the coast give some of the best views of these islands: Inchkeith, Inchcolm, Inchmickery and Inchgarvie.

Of these, the best known is

Starley Burn Falls

possibly the small island of Inchcolm, set just off the coast from Aberdour, and a popular visitor attraction, particularly in the summer months. The long and varied history of the island is said to reach back to the Dark Ages, and the Abbey, which remains on the island is thought to have been built on the site of an earlier Abbey, possibly dating back to before the 12th century. The religious significance of the island was firmly established by David I in 1235 when the status of abbey was bestowed on the buildings. These buildings, among the best-preserved medieval ruins in Scotland, are now under the care of Historic Scotland and can be visited from between April and October each year. Much later in its history, Inchcolm was fortified during the First and Second World Wars, in order to provide vital defences to Edinburgh and to the naval base further along the coastline at Rosyth, and some evidence of this role can still be seen on the island to this day.

Perhaps better known for its wartime role however, is the Island of Inchgarvie, which together with Inchcolm and the tiny island of Inchmickery, was used throughout both world wars.

The island of Inchgarvie lies almost directly beneath the Forth Bridge and has a long history of a defensive role; dating back to the Middle Ages. And although the role of the island was set to change forever when the foundations for the Forth Bridge were placed on the island, these plans changed following the Tay Bridge disaster and the foundations were never put to use.

Inchgarvie was, however, to fulfil a significant role during wartime in defending nearby Edinburgh and Rosyth Dockyards from both air and submarine attacks. Gun emplacements on the island and Inchmickery were manned throughout the war years and the buildings can still be seen quite clearly both from the coastline and from the bird's-eye view provided from the bridges.

The terrain of the two islands, together with the clever construction of the fortifications gives the low lying islands the appearance of battleships – a sinister sight on a dark evening, but one said to be highly effective during the war years.

This military history is one that is echoed by the island of Inchkeith. This island, which has similar volcanic geology to that of the nearby Bass Rock, has been inhabited throughout the centuries, but has had a long and varied history often coloured by conflict and battle – most likely due to its close proximity to Edinburgh. Like many of the other islands of the Forth, the earliest reference to the island can be traced back to the 12th century, when those making the often arduous journey up the Forth used the island as a stopover. During the volatile 14th century, the island fell repeatedly under attack and it is thought that this was because of its location, en route to the significant battlefields of Central Scotland. The history of the island also has some more curious stories to it: from the late 15th century the island was brought into use as a quarantine, taking sufferers of a contagious disease known as grandgore – thought by some sources to be syphilis – from nearby Edinburgh to the island where they were to remain while 'God provided for their health'.

Inchkeith was also once the site of a bizarre language experiment. Historian Robert Lyndsay of Pitscottie is attributed as having recorded that in 1493, King James IV ordered the undertaking of an experiment to discover the true or 'original' language of mankind. This involved the transportation of a deaf-mute woman, along with her two infant children, to the isolated island of Inchkeith. King James is said to have believed that freed from the bounds of normal society the children would speak the language of the Gods. The children, it is said, returned from the island a number of years later, still mute. Thankfully, their story along with the varied and fascinating history of the other islands that lie in the western reaches of the Forth is documented and continues to provide intrigue even in the 21st century.

LOCAL BUSINESSES

DALGETY BAY

Food and beverage

Dining Fine Takeaway, Bay Centre, Regents Way, Dalgety Bay, KY11 9YD. Tel: 01383 825881

Marini's Takeaway, Bay Centre, Regents Way, Dalgety Bay, KY11 9YD. Tel: 01383 824466

The Bay Inn, Regents Way, Dalgety Bay, KY11 9UY, Tel: 01383 820903

RS McColl Newsagents, Bay Centre, Regents Way, Dalgety Bay, KY11 9YD. Tel: 01383 820903

Tesco Supermarket, Bay Centre, Regents Way, Dalgety Bay, KY11 9YD. Tel: 08456779237

Medical

Rowland Pharmacy, Bay Centre, Regents Way, Dalgety Bay, KY11 9UY. Tel: 01383 824257

Banks

ATM, Bay Centre, Regents Way, Dalgety Bay, KY11 9UY

The facilities are not directly on the path.

ABERDOUR

Accommodation

The Chaumer Self Catering Cottage, Barns Farm, Aberdour, KY3 0RY. Tel: 01383 823872, www.barnsfarm.info

Riverview Farmhouse Flat, Dalachy Farm, Aberdour, KY3 0RY. Tel: 01383 860340, www.dalchy.co.uk

Seaside Place B&B, 21 Seaside Place, Aberdour, KY3 0TX. Tel: 01383 860197, www.aberdourseasideplacebandb.co.uk

Aberdour Hotel, 38 High Street, Aberdour, KY3 0SW. Tel: 01383 860325, www.aberdourhotel.co.uk (Welcome Port)

Woodside Hotel, 78 High Street, Aberdour, KY3 0SW. Tel: 01383 860328, www.thewoodsidehotel.co.uk (Welcome port)

Forthview Hotel, Hawcraig Point, Aberdour, KY3 0TZ. Tel: 01383 860402, www.forthviewhotel.co.uk

The Cedar Inn, 20 Shore Street, Aberdour, KY3 0TR. Tel: 01383 860310, www.thecedarinn.co.uk

Food and Beverage

FC Lonie Bakers, High Street, Aberdour, KY3 0SW. Tel: 01383 860330

Aberdour General Store, 21 High Street, Aberdour, KY3 0SH Tel: 01383 861180

Jack's Newsagents, High Street, Aberdour, KY3 0SW.

Foresters Arms, 35 High Street, Aberdour, KY3 0SW Tel: 01383 860544

Miriam's Tea and Coffee Shop, 16 Shore Road, Aberdour, KY3 0TR. Tel: 01383 860544

Aberdour Castle Tea Room, Aberdour Castle, Aberdour, KY3 0SL. Tel: 01383 860519

Room with a View Restaurant, Hawkcraig Point, Aberdour, KY10 3EA. Tel: 01383 860402 www. roomwithaviewrestaurant.co.uk

Post Office

Aberdour Post Office, 45 High Street, Aberdour, KY3 0SW

Banks

ATM, High Street, Aberdour, KY3 0SW

LOCAL BUSINESSES

ABERDOUR

Galleries and Gift Shops

Mystique Moments, 59-61 High Street, Aberdour, KY3 0SJ. Tel: 01383 860160

The Quay Gallery, The Shore, Aberdour, KY3 0TY. Tel: 01383 860602

Out of this World, Gift Shop, 12 High Street, Aberdour, KY3 0SW. Tel: 01383 860862

Antiques and Gifts, 25 High Street, Aberdour, KY3 0SW. Tel: 01383 860523

BURNTISLAND

Accommodation

69 Cromwell Road B&B, 69 Cromwell Road, Burntisland, KY3 9EL. Tel: 01592 874969, www.69cromwellroad.co.uk

Links Guest House, 45 Kinghorn Road, Burntisland, KY3 9EB. Tel: 01592 874037

Gruinard Guest House, 148 Kinghorn Road, Burntisland, KY3 9JU. Tel: 01592 873877, www.gruinardguesthouse.co.uk

Kingswood Hotel, Kinghorn Road, Burntisland, KY3 9LL. Tel: 01592 872329, www.kingswoodhotel.co.uk

Sands Hotel, Lochies Road, Burntisland, KY3 9JX. Tel: 01592 872230, www.burntislandsands.co.uk

Hotel Inchview Hotel, 69 Kinghorn Road, Burntisland, KY3 9EB. Tel: 01592 872239, www.inchview.co.uk

Burntisland Holiday Lets, Burntisland, Tel: 0131 467 9379, www.burntislandholidaylets.com

Food and Beverage

The Star Pub, 73 High Street, Burntisland, Tel: 01592 873130

Potter About, Ceramic Café, 253A

Artis Gallery, 33 High Street, Aberdour, KY3 0SW. Tel: 01383 860705

Hearts Desire, 7 Shore Road, Aberdour, KY3 0TR. Tel: 01383 860124

Medical

Aberdour Pharmacy, 30 High Street, Aberdour, KY3 0SW. Tel: 01383 860474

Tourist Attractions

Aberdour Castle, Garden and Tearooms, Aberdour, KY3 0SL. Tel: 01383 860519 www.historic-scotland.gov.uk

High Street, Burntisland, KY3 9AQ. Tel: 01592 873860, www.potterabout.co.uk

Friendlies Takeaway, 164 High Street, Burntisland, KY3 9AP. Tel: 01592 870444

Glen Bakers, 223 High Street, Burntisland, KY3 9AE. Tel: 01592 873774

Golf Tavern, 17 Links Place, Burntisland, KY3 9DY. Tel: 01592 873884

Links Fish Bar, 18 Links Place, Burntisland, KY3 9DY. Tel: 01592 873001

Cafe Inspire, Beacon Leisure Centre, Burntisland, KY3 9BS. Tel: 01592 872211

Costcutter Convenience Store, 229 High Street, Burntisland, KY3 9AE. Tel: 01592 873374 www.costcutter.com

Food for Thought Café, 267 High Street, Burntisland, KY3 9AQ

Mario's Pizza and Kebab House, 175 High Street, Burntisland, KY3 9AE. Tel: 01592 872757

Old Port Bar, 277 High Street, Burntisland, KY3 9AQ. Tel: 01592 872681

Peach Blossom Takeaway, 197 High Street, Burntisland, KY3 9AE. Tel: 01592 872372

Ramano's Fish Bar, 144a High Street, Burntisland, KY3 9AP. Tel: 01592 874200

LOCAL BUSINESSES

BURNTISLAND

Food and Beverage (cont)

The Silver Tassie Pub, 86 High Street, Burntisland, KY3 9AS.
Tel: 01592 873469

Smugglers Inn, 14 Harbour Place, Burntisland, KY3 9DP. Tel: 01592 873882

Tikasam Takeway, 179 High Street, Burntisland, KY3 9AW.
Tel: 01592 870055

Waverley Café, 263 High Street, Burntisland, KY3 9AQ. Tel: 01592 874658

Londis Convenience Store, 122 High Street, Burntisland, KY3 9AP.
Tel: 01592 872283

RT Stuart Bakers and Café, 186 High Street, Burntisland, Fife, KY3 9AP.
Tel: 01592 873726

Post Office

Burntisland Post Office, 192-196 High Street, Burntisland, KY3 9AH

Bank

ATM, High Street, Burntisland, KY3 9UW

Medical

Lloyds Pharmacy, 239 High Street, Burntisland, KY3 9UW.
Tel: 01592 873725
www.lloydspharmacy.com

Galleries and Gift Shops

Fair Shares Gift Shop, 128 High Street, Burntisland, KY3 9AP.
Tel: 01592 870071

Tourist Attractions

Heritage Walks, Burntisland Heritage Trust, 4 Kirkgate, Burntisland.
Tel: 01592 872121
www.burntisland.net

Beacon Leisure Centre, Lammerlaws Road, Burntisland, KY3 9BS.
Tel: 01592 872211
www.fifeleisure.org.uk

Museum of Communication, 131 High Street, Burntisland, KY3 9AA.
Tel: 01592 874836 www.mocft.co.uk

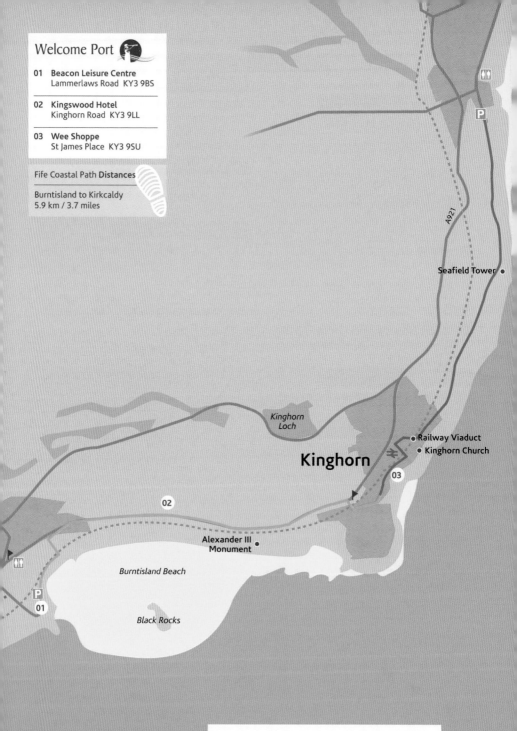

Welcome Port

01 **Beacon Leisure Centre**
   Lammerlaws Road KY3 9BS

02 **Kingswood Hotel**
   Kinghorn Road KY3 9LL

03 **Wee Shoppe**
   St James Place KY3 9SU

Fife Coastal Path **Distances**

Burntisland to Kirkcaldy
5.9 km / 3.7 miles

Seafield Tower

A921

Kinghorn
Loch

Kinghorn

Railway Viaduct
Kinghorn Church

03

02

Alexander III
Monument

Burntisland Beach

01

Black Rocks

Burntisland to Kirkcaldy

CHAPTER SEVEN

BURNTISLAND TO KIRKCALDY

STARTING at The Beacon Leisure Centre, Burntisland, this section of the Fife Coastal Path is 5 miles (8 km) long and includes historic towns, botanically important coastal grasslands and much of geological interest.

Burntisland's history is recorded as far back as Roman times, when Agricola sailed into the harbour in AD83. Burntisland became a Royal Burgh in 1541 and was used as a Naval Port during the reign of James V. The town was besieged by Cromwell in 1651 and eventually fell to him. It was also home to the world's first Railway Ferry in 1850 where the wagons were loaded onto boats with rail lines built into the deck. The ferry crossing took the passengers over the Forth to Granton where the journey continued by train. This service ran successfully until the 1890s when the Forth Bridge was completed, allowing trains to cross the Forth without the need for the ferry crossing. Today, the town has a good beach and promenade and a fair is held on the Links every year.

The path from Burntisland to Kinghorn is mainly road walking, but gives fine views to the shore. We wanted the path, as far as possible, to be accessible at all states of the tide, so we couldn't put it right at the shore because it would have disappeared at high tide.

You may want to stop and take in the monument that marks the place where Alexander III died in 1286, and while you do, look out over the expanse of sand that runs from Burntisland to Pettycur Harbour. This sand is a rich feeding ground for wading birds during the winter when quite large flocks can gather.

Kinghorn is a small picturesque village but was once a Royal Burgh of importance, used by various kings. Unfortunately, none of the fine buildings associated with them now remain. It is pleasing to see that the Town Hall has recently been restored.

The Fife Historic Buildings Trust restored Kinghorn Town Hall in 2009 and now has its offices there. The Town Hall is a wonderful example of early 19th century civic pride but fell into disrepair in the 1980s. The restoration included the creation of a three-bedroom holiday apartment on the first and second floors. The first floor includes a magnificent main hall with south facing windows and two original fireplaces. For further details about the apartment please visit the Vivat Trust website: www.vivat-trust.org.

The harbour is believed to date from the 18th century. The town had a ferry terminal at Pettycur that linked both sides of the Forth and was operational until the late 18th century. The prominent prow overlooking Pettycur Bay is where witches were burned and is called 'Witches Hill'. Kinghorn Church, dating

Kinghorn Church dating back to 1774 is worth a visit

originally from 1774 is certainly worth visiting.

Leaving Kinghorn, the path goes through coastal grassland in which uncommon plants such as bloody cranesbill, rockrose, agrimony and wild clary all grow. Not far out of Kinghorn, note the small well on the left surrounded in periwinkle, where past travellers were refreshed.

The geology of the coast here is interesting as some of the rocks came from lava flows, the result of an eruption from the Binn Hill volcano about 300 million years ago. Layers of limestone lie under these lava flows and they are a rich source of fossils of the sea life of a time when Scotland (then at the Equator) had a tropical climate.

I often bring school groups to this area to do a fossil hunt and to talk about Fife's volcanic history. One of the problems I have is to get across the timescale involved when I'm talking to the boys and girls. If 300 million years ago is difficult enough for adults to comprehend, it's much more difficult when you are only nine years old. I knew I had failed with one group when a young lad came up to me afterwards and said: 'You know the last time the volcano erupted – well my Dad just got out in time!'.

At the point where Seafield Tower comes into view, look directly down on to the coast and you will see the remains of two limekilns and seals basking on the rocks just offshore. Between the Tower and the next car park is new housing built on the site of the old Seafield Colliery. The wall out to sea is the remains of a harbour that was built in 1889, but never used.

Bloody cranesbill is an uncommon plant that can be seen on the path

Did You Know?
Blue Flag Beaches

It might not be the largest county in Scotland by any measurement, but when it comes to beaches, Fife punches well above its weight, with over 100 miles of coastline dotted with award-winning beaches. The majority of Scotland's blue flag beaches are in Fife and a number of beaches in the area also hold Seaside Awards, ensuring that if you're heading to the east with your bucket and spade you're guaranteed to find a beautiful beach, safe in the knowledge that it's reached the highest possible standards for visitors. A Blue Flag is the highest possible accolade that can be awarded to a beach. Run by not-for-profit organisation the Foundation for Environmental Education, over 3,650 flags have been awarded to beaches and marinas in 44 countries across the world.

In Scotland, the Blue Flag programme is operated by Keep Scotland Beautiful, which ensures that awards are only made to beaches that attain the required standards of water quality, environmental management, education and information and safety. Reaching these high standards is no mean feat.

Beaches achieving the water quality standards required to win a Blue Flag must comply not only with levels required for the water tests, but also the level and frequency of water monitoring required. The environmental management criteria cover a wide range of issues, from the cleanliness of the beach to the toilet

The remains of one of two limekilns on the shore

facilities available and the restrictions for dogs on the beach.

Education and information standards ensure that adequate signage must be placed on the beach to cover everything from maps of the facilities on the beach to specialised information on the ecology of the local area and bathing water quality. But, for many families visiting Blue Flag beaches, the reassurance that they have reached the required high standards is a major factor – ensuring adequate life-guarding, robust emergency procedures and careful management of beach events.

With these challenging criteria in mind, it is not surprising that Fife is very proud to have been the first recipient of Scotland's first Blue Flag Award, at Aberdour Silver Sands and has maintained it ever since.

Meeting the standards required by the Seaside Awards – now approaching their 20th year – is just as demanding with 28 criteria to be met by resort beaches and 14 by rural beaches. This essential distinction between resort and rural is made in recognition of the very different beach experiences offered, often in close proximity, by beaches in Scotland.

The Seaside Awards cover everything from litter management to information provision and safety procedures to water quality. Keep Scotland Beautiful describe Resort Seaside Award beaches as being those which are 'usually actively promoted to encourage visitors and are within easy access of developed facilities', while rural seaside award beaches 'must be clean and promote sustainable behaviour on information boards, provide maps and have appropriate safety management'.

Community involvement is also encouraged. With so much beautiful and well-maintained coastline, it's not surprising that Fife beaches are recognised in both categories with six rural and six resort award winners.

Recognition of the quality of Fife's beaches and all that they can offer is – rightly – a great source of pride to many in the area. In spite of the challenges brought about by the legacy of heavy industry in the area, current funding difficulties and the uncertainty of a changing climate, there remains a determination to ensure that the beaches of Fife are able to offer great opportunities for leisure and recreation, sustainable tourism, and enjoyment for all those who visit.

And with generations of Scots still misty-eyed about childhood holidays spent in Fife decades ago, when endless days were whiled away on the beach at places like Aberdour, Burntisland, Lower Largo or St Andrews, it's not hard to understand why.

LOCAL BUSINESSES

KINGHORN

Accommodation

Hideaway Beach House, 107 Pettycur Road, Kinghorn, KY3 9RW. Tel: 01592 892535
www.hideawaybeach.co.uk

Salmon Cottage Holiday Let, 27 St James Place, Kinghorn, KY3 9SU. Tel: 0161 456 1147
www.salmoncottage.co.uk

The Wee Hoose Self Catering, 6-8 Nethergate, Kinghorn, KY3 9SY. Tel: 01592 891074

Carousel Motel B&B, Pettycur Road, Kinghorn, KY3 9RN. Tel: 01592 890577

Food and Beverage

The Crown Tavern, 55 High Street, Kinghorn, KY3 9UW. Tel: 01592 890340

The Ship Tavern, 2 Bruce Street, Kinghorn, KY3 9TJ. Tel: 01592 890655 (Welcome Port)

The Auld Hoose, 6-8 Nethergate, Kinghorn, KY3 9SY. Tel: 01592 891074

Fortune House Takeaway, 10 Rossland Place, Kinghorn, KY3 9SS. Tel: 01592 890842

Niven's Coffee Shop, 49 High Street, Kinghorn, KY3 9UW. Tel: 01592 890111

Costcutter Convenience Store, 3 Rossland Place, Kinghorn, KY3 9TU

RT Stuart Bakers, 32 High Street, Kinghorn, KY3 9UE. Tel: 01592 890576

The Wee Shoppe, 29 St James Place, Kinghorn, KY3 9SU. Tel: 01592 891677 (Welcome Port)

Co-op Store, 26-28 High Street, Kinghorn, Fife, KY3 9UE. Tel: 01592 890289

Medical

Lloyds Pharmacy, 63 High Street, Kinghorn, KY3 9UW. Tel: 01592 890209, www.lloydspharmacy.com

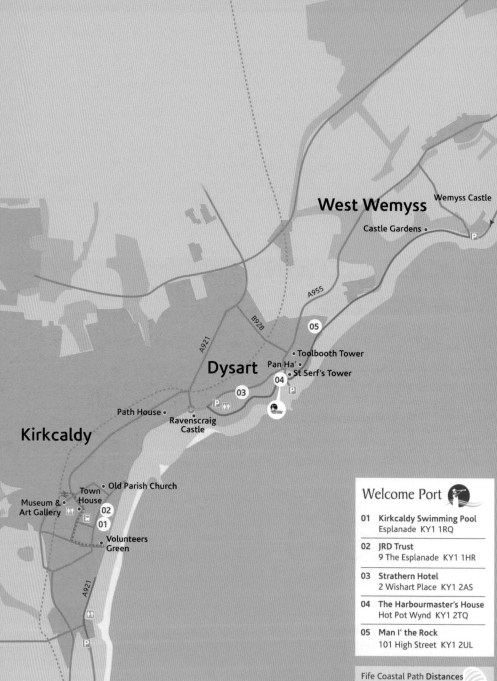

West Wemyss

Wemyss Castle

Castle Gardens

A955

B928

05

A921

Dysart

Toolbooth Tower

Pan Ha'

St Serf's Tower

03

04

Path House

Ravenscraig
Castle

Kirkcaldy

Old Parish Church

Town
House

Museum &
Art Gallery

02

01

Volunteers
Green

A921

Welcome Port

01 **Kirkcaldy Swimming Pool**
    Esplanade KY1 1RQ

02 **JRD Trust**
    9 The Esplanade KY1 1HR

03 **Strathern Hotel**
    2 Wishart Place KY1 2AS

04 **The Harbourmaster's House**
    Hot Pot Wynd KY1 2TQ

05 **Man I' the Rock**
    101 High Street KY1 2UL

Fife Coastal Path Distances

Kirkcaldy to West Wemyss
8.5 km / 4.2 miles

Kirkcaldy to West Wemyss

CHAPTER EIGHT

KIRKCALDY TO WEST WEMYSS

FROM the Seafield Car Park in Kirkcaldy to West Wemyss is 4.5 miles (6.6 km) and takes in historic buildings, picturesque villages, industrial heritage and interesting birdlife in the winter. We also take a break at the Harbourmaster's House in Dysart along the way.

Kirkcaldy is known as the 'Lang Toun' due to its four-mile long Main Street. It was originally home to textiles and salt industries but enjoyed greater prosperity in the late 19th and early 20th century as home of the linoleum industry. Kirkcaldy also has a wonderful Museum and Art gallery that is well worth a visit.

Why not spend a while exploring the town before continuing your journey by heading back down to the Coast? Kirkcaldy Esplanade was built by unemployed men and originally completed in 1923. At times, the sea can still come over the wall and flood the esplanade. Beyond the esplanade lies Kirkcaldy Harbour which was once busy serving the town's linoleum industry. On the other side of the road lies the white building known as Sailors Walk, which is said to date from 1459 and is the oldest in Kirkcaldy.

Beyond Path House at the top of the hill, a road leads to Pathhead Sands, an important roosting area for wading birds during winter, so a worthwhile detour from the path.

Looking up, there is an impressive view of Ravenscraig Castle, built by James II

The remains of Ravenscraig Castle

Above is the harbour at Dysart circa 1860 and below, the harbour circa 1897

The Harbourmaster's House, Dysart is now HQ of the Fife Coast and Countryside Trust

and dating from 1460. The castle was never completed as planned as James II died in battle, so the castle was redesigned to be smaller for his wife to live in. The rock, on which it is built, is both red and yellow sandstone. The Castle itself can be accessed from Ravenscraig Park, an area gifted to the town by the Nairn family, the largest of the linoleum makers in the area who made their money from this industry. The Park also has a 16th century beehive 'doocot' and the Sailors Walk.

Beyond the Park lies the picturesque village of Dysart, whose history goes back to the beginning of Christianity in Scotland through an association with St Serf. The tower named after him is all that remains of a 13th century church and it stands close to the restored cottages of Pan Ha' – a name which relates to the saltpans which once occupied the shore area. At that time, salt was worth more per weight than gold, and it was exported to the Continent via Holland.

While you are in Dysart, be sure to visit the Harbourmaster's House. The building houses a fabulous Coastal Visitor Centre and a lovely bistro serving a mouth-watering variety of food and drinks. The building is also home to Fife Coast and Countryside Trust who manage, maintain and promote the Fife Coastal Path.

The Harbourmaster's House has been standing at the foot of Hot Pot Wynd at Dysart Harbour since around 1840, taking the place of a much earlier Shore House which was demolished in 1796.

Looking at the peaceful harbour today with its fleet of small boats, it's hard to imagine what it was like when it was an important and very busy commercial port. That's when tall-masted sailing ships from foreign ports were packed so tightly that it was possible to walk across their decks from one side of the dock to the other. There was a brisk import and export trade with the Low Countries and the Baltic, with the tall ships bringing in a wide and varied amount of goods and taking away locally produced coal, salt and other items.

Although Dysart was recorded as a port as early as 1450, there was no real harbour, only a jetty in the bay opposite the houses at Pan Ha'. This gradually fell into disrepair, but the foundation stones can still be seen at low water at the largest spring tides three or four times a year. The present harbour was created in the early 17th century when an east pier was built, with the overall structure being added to and changed by successive generations.

The ground floor of the Harbourmaster's House was used to store a varied amount of imported goods, as well as holding items that were exported from Fife. It must have had some of the sounds and scents of an eastern bazaar, as some of the items stored were oak bark, apples and onions, wine and spirits, timber, linseed oil, pantiles for Dysart roofs, flax, clay for Kirkcaldy potteries, tallow for candles, and books.

There was a wide range of goods leaving Dysart for other ports: salt to Aberdeen and Inverness, bales of cloth to Leith, and tons upon tons of coal mined locally and brought down to the harbour by a never-ending stream of horses and carts.

In those days the building was three storeys high, before the pier was built up in front of it to cater for loading larger ships. It was also home to the harbourmaster, who played a key role in the activity of the harbour and who was given the accommodation rent-free as part of his wages.

The post of harbourmaster carried important duties: he recorded the time that each incoming ship came in and allocated their berths and put them into position in the inner dock and harbour. He also had to supervise the working of the dock gates, and collect the harbour dues that went to Dysart Town Council (before the amalgamation with Kirkcaldy in 1930) towards the upkeep of the harbour. The coal company owned by the Earl of Rosslyn (who lived in Dysart House, now the Carmelite Monastery) was paid per ton by customers ordering coal.

The old Dysart Town Council minutes from the mid-1800s show a steady procession of harbourmasters, some of whom ended their careers in a variety of sorry circumstances. Probably the most dramatic was in 1900 when the harbourmaster left the dock sluice gates open after high water, and the schooner Speculator was badly damaged. Lawyers' letters flew between the town council and the ship's owners, who finally accepted £100 in compensation, a fair amount in those days.

There was also the opportunity – as in any public office where there are cash transactions – to be less than honest with the harbour dues, a discrepancy which was brought to light when a second check on the coal tonnage was made by the weighman.

The first man to be recorded in the post was John Robertson, who was appointed around 1850, followed in fairly quick succession by Thomas Turnbull, Andrew Dick, David Hume and then Captain Andrew Thomson, who resigned in 1882. When Captain Thomson left his post, the Fifeshire Advertiser newspaper of the time reported: 'Twelve applications for the office of harbourmaster were submitted to the Town Council meeting, and the Council appointed Mr John Harrow to fill the office.'

Four years later, the council considered Mr Harrow's application for a rise, again the local paper reported: 'An application had been received from Mr Harrow, harbourmaster, for an increase of salary. His present salary was £1 weekly, with free house. He was a very attentive man, and the Provost was not against him receiving an increase, although the work had been done by Mr Hume at a very small salary and had given great satisfaction, as had Captain Thomson, and he did not think the duties were increased.'

One councillor thought he should receive a little increase, as his wages were not large. Another pointed out that the harbourmaster must be up at all the tides and that he did his work well. After a prolonged discussion, it was agreed to increase his wages by two shillings a week. The rise, though not excessive, must have been enough to satisfy John Harrow who retired in 1900 at a good age.

He had in fact tried to retire previously but was persuaded to stay on, to the detriment of his health. Edwin Coatsworth, who was often seen accompanied by his dog Toby, succeeded him.

In 1906 Andrew Dryburgh, one of the most notable of Dysart's

Andrew Dryburgh: Dysart Harbourmaster and ship's carpenter on the Cutty Sark harbourmasters, was appointed. There was a shipbuilding yard at the harbour at that time, which built and then later repaired ships, and as a young man he served his apprenticeship there.

He then enlisted for the crew of the newly built clipper, Cutty Sark on her maiden voyage as carpenter's mate, finishing up as ship's carpenter. He lived in Vancouver Island for nine years where he must have got on to a sound financial footing, as on his return to Dysart, he bought over the same shipyard where he had started his working life, as well as taking on the harbourmaster's post.

The last harbourmaster to be employed by Dysart Town Council, and the last to occupy the house was William Geldart.

There was an even quicker turnover of pilots, who were employed by Trinity House and who were not under the jurisdiction of the Town Council.

Although there must have been a good number of pilots who carried out their duties carefully and honestly, it is believed there were a few rogues. Some pilots were fined for letting ships run aground, or for refusing to take ships out of the harbour.

There was a set scale of charges for ships coming in and out of the harbour, but the pilots could ask the ships' masters (especially those who were new to the port) for an inflated fee and then pocket the difference. With perhaps a dozen ships a week going in or out of the harbour, some of the pilots, if tempted, could make a sizeable income with their extra charges. It's believed a few took advantage of the scheme and spent most of the extra cash they made in the local pubs.

This practice was tried out once too often by Thomas Cairns, a colourful character whose pilot's licence was withdrawn twice for 'violent and outrageous conduct', but who was reinstated after a successful petition signed by 300 local people. His scheme to get more than the standard charges from visitors met with some opposition from a Danish skipper who objected strongly and produced a revolver to underline his disapproval. Cairns knocked the revolver out of his hand, but the skipper went down to his cabin and appeared with a rifle. By that time Cairns and his companion had jumped into their own small boat and rowed to safety pursued by shots from the captain.

Ships which came in without cargoes were loaded with ballast such as stones and large boulders, often tipped overboard or removed by horse and cart and dumped on the beach: even today there are pieces of rocks on the foreshore which started off in the fjords of Norway.

The off-loaded stones began to block up the harbour, and a tunnel was built through the cliff face with rails laid down for trucks to take away the ballast. The tunnel is still there, although the ground level has been raised over the years, making a passage between the harbour and the start of Pathhead sands.

Kirkcaldy folk spent a lot of their leisure time going along to Dysart Harbour to watch the busy scene. 'It was quite a Sunday expedition with your parents and the family, to go along Sailors' Walk where you were level with the top of the masts of all the boats that were in Dysart dock,' said one elderly man, recalling days in the early 20th century.

'It would be so full of ships that you wondered how they ever got them in or out. They were packed in and every space seemed to be filled up. They were in for coal, and the Dysart pit was just a few hundred yards along so the horses and carts brought the coal down. A carter would bring along two horses and his two carts to the big chute at the side, and he just emptied his cart straight down into the hold.'

And a great-grandmother remembered as a very small girl being taken for a walk with her grandfather every weekend to the harbour to see the ships in the dock. 'I looked over the side of the harbour and saw the coal chutes going down into the ships,' she said. 'One day I lost my balance and slid down one of the chutes, but my grandfather got me back up again.'

The huts at the end of the harbour were originally the premises of the Dysart Swimming Club and Humane Society, formed in 1888 to teach local youngsters to swim – a necessary skill for youngsters who played near the edge of the dock.

The buildings were used as changing huts, with separate accommodation for men and women in those Victorian times. During World War I, soldiers were billeted in the huts and the harbour was out of bounds to civilians during the war. Two other small buildings still stand nearby – the pilots' hut facing the dock gates, and the stowers' bothy for the men who shovelled coal into the waiting boats.

In a bid to attract bigger ships, the dock was cleaned out and deepened in 1924. Unfortunately, this proved to be counter-productive, as the temporary closure of the harbour attracted ships to Burntisland, or Methil docks instead. Fife Coal Company, which was then the major user of the harbour, refused to reimburse Dysart Town Council for the work done – a catastrophic financial blow.

This was quickly followed by the closure of the Lady Blanche pit for economic reasons, and in 1929 the harbour was closed as a commercial port and there was no further need for a harbourmaster.

It lay virtually unused for 20 years and it seemed unlikely that it would ever be open to ships again. The very existence of the harbour was under threat in the early 1960s, when there was a proposal by Kirkcaldy Town Council to fill it in completely.

Fortunately, the tide turned in 1967, when the harbour was taken over by the newly formed Dysart Sailing Club who restored it to full use for small boats after many years of hard and determined work by club members. The club then employed Will Carr in 1972 as harbourmaster, a post he held until he was over

80. Although the boats he dealt with were a different size than the tall-masted sailing ships of his childhood, he remembered them well. 'When I was a lad, I remember seeing the harbour full of sailing ships,' he recalled. 'They had to enter port under sail with the tide, and it was a great thing to see those three-masted big ships with their crew scampering through the rigging. There would be maybe eight tall ships in port, with two or three others anchored in the Forth waiting to get in.

'There were a lot of foreign ships such as the Herald, a Norwegian ship that made the fastest sailing ever from Norway in 48 hours – well, that's what the crew told us anyhow.

'When a ship needed repair, it had to be pulled out of the water by a big wheel with cogs, and chains which were thicker than my arm attached to the ship. It took a dozen men to walk round this great wheel to move the cogs. They said that by the time the ship was pulled on to the land, the men had walked the equivalent distance as from here to Burntisland and back again.'

By that time, the Harbourmaster's House had undergone a change in use. Mrs Geldart, widow of the last harbourmaster, still occupied part of the house until the mid-1950s. By the early 1960s, part of the building was used as the premises of Archibald Shanks, firewood merchant, while a young art student used part of the cellar as his makeshift studio. Shortly afterwards, Dysart Sailing Club leased the building to use as its clubhouse, and members had space to build and repair their boats, with the upper floor being used to spread out sails to dry.

By 1994 however it was becoming obvious that the building was becoming dangerous and needed a lot of work to put right. The upper floors were riddled with dry rot and the general condition of the building was deteriorating.

The sailing club agreed to move their headquarters to the nearby 'Oil Shed' and for some years there were very real fears for the future safety of the building as it was left empty at the mercy of the elements, vandals and an ever-growing colony of pigeons.

Initial plans in 1996 by a whisky company to convert it into offices, flats and a heritage centre fell through. However, in 2000 as part of a new Regeneration Initiative, the first stage began to renovate the B-listed building, when work started to strip out the interior and make the exterior windproof and water-tight, funded by Fife Council and Fife Enterprise.

Two years later, applications were invited from firms, or individuals to either buy or lease the Harbourmaster's House and turn it into a viable business concern. Interest was shown for a wide variety of uses, including luxury holiday apartments, artists' workshops and gallery, a restaurant and lounge, Scottish music centre, loft apartments, and offices.

None of the plans were suitable, mainly because at that stage, the start-up costs

The Interpretation Centre in the Harbourmaster's House offering visitors a chance to learn about Dysart and the Fife Coastal Path

for a business in a building, which had neither floors nor services, would have been prohibitive.

The turning point came when Amanda McFarlane, the Chief Executive of Fife Coast and Countryside Trust, which was then based temporarily in Leven, was walking along the Fife Coastal Path.

Her attention was struck by the empty building at the edge of the harbour and there and then she decided that this would be the perfect place for the Trust's permanent headquarters. After a lengthy consultation process involving Fife Council, Fife Coast and Countryside Trust, and local voluntary organisations, the Dysart Trust and Dysart Regeneration Forum, a massive £1m redevelopment programme was put in place.

Work started in October 2005 to transform the building into offices, interpretation centre, community room and bistro.

The work was not without its challenges. The interior of the building had to be gutted and fitted out from scratch with modern technology, disabled access, a glass lift, kitchen and toilets. A time capsule with information on Dysart past and present gathered by the Dysart Trust and local primary school children was sealed in one of the walls.

The renovated building was officially opened in September 2006 by the

Above, The Harbour Bistro on the ground floor of the building and below, visitors enjoying the hospitality and unique views of Dysart's historic harbour

Right Honourable Gordon Brown (then Chancellor of the Exchequer and MP for Kirkcaldy and Cowdenbeath), and Patsy Curran, great-granddaughter of harbourmaster Andrew Dryburgh. Patsy also brought with her the tiny doll that Andrew had brought back with him from the maiden voyage of the Cutty Sark.

Since then, the Harbourmaster's House has gone from strength to strength, with several awards including a Gold Award in the Green Business Tourism Scheme and a 4-Star visitor attraction award from Visit Scotland. It has become an integral part of the Fife Coastal Path for thousands of visitors, many of whom have been inspired by the displays in the interpretation centre showing the beauty spots on the 117 mile walk from Kincardine to Newburgh and learned something of the history of Dysart and its harbour, before sampling the delights of the bistro overlooking the water.

The harbourmasters of yesterday would surely have been pleased to see their old building still playing an important part in today's harbour life, allowing visitors and local people to appreciate the beauty of this historic part of Fife.

Hopefully now that you are refreshed and have enjoyed your stop at the Harbourmaster's House, it is time to continue your journey along the coast. Leaving Dysart, the path goes through the remains of the disused Frances Colliery, a pit whose working coal seams went underneath the Forth. The area of bing material, which goes down to the shore, is already being reclaimed by nature, with teasel colonising the spoil.

After going through the woodland at Blair Point, the path drops down to sea level and is a good point to watch sea ducks during the winter. Eider is especially common, but red-breasted mergansers are normally seen as well as my favourite of the winter-visiting ducks, the beautiful long-tailed duck.

Beyond the Chapel Garden, the private burial ground for the Wemyss family, look for the blocked off entrance to a tunnel through the red sandstone rock. This tunnel was a link to the Hugo Pit at Coaltown of Wemyss. It has been blocked off for safety reasons.

Fulmars are usually present on the sandstone cliffs as you enter the village of West Wemyss. Although fulmars look a bit like gulls, they are actually related to albatrosses.

Their legs are set far back on their bodies which makes it almost impossible for them to walk. They push off from the cliffs and hope then to catch an updraught that they can soar away on.

Every year without doubt, when the newborns make their first flight, there is always one that fails to soar away and finds itself landing on the ground, unable to walk to the water. That's when my phone rings with people thinking the bird is injured. I go down, check the bird isn't injured, pick it up and put it back on an appropriate spot somewhere high to let it try again.

It can be rewarding to give a bird a second chance, but actually, in the case of fulmars, I hate it. My reason for that odd view? The young bird doesn't understand that I'm trying to help it so tries to defend itself by spitting foul-smelling oil at me. Mostly I can dodge it, but sometimes they get a bull's-eye, and no one will come near me for the rest of the day.

Did You Know?
Linoleum Industry

If asked to think of the major industries of Fife, what would you come up with?

Mining – possibly. Fishing – almost definitely. Linoleum – probably not. But, at one time, the town of Kirkcaldy was the biggest manufacturer of linoleum in the world.

At its peak in the late 19th century business was booming to such an extent that six factories were hard at work across the town and an estimated 3,000 people were employed in its production and associated industry.

Englishman Frederick Walton who aimed to create an alternative to Indian rubber using solidified linseed oil first undertook the production of linoleum in the early 19th century. The process was refined many times to produce the floor covering we now know as linoleum, with Walton deriving its name from the Latin of its two main ingredients: linum (linen or flax) and oleum (oil).

Although Frederick Walton had patented his product, his early work had inspired Kirkcaldy-born entrepreneur Michael Nairn. Michael Nairn was already experienced in producing canvas for sailcloth, but with demand for sailcloth in decline, in 1847 he opened a factory in the town of Pathhead to manufacture canvas for the floor cloth industry. Although Michael Nairn died in 1858 the Fifer's canny son recognised an opportunity and when Walton's linoleum patent expired in 1876, the Fife operation soon flourished into a major success, bringing prosperity to Kirkcaldy and also further afield.

A 1956 government-commissioned report on the supply of linoleum shows just how far the influence of Michael Nairn & Co Ltd was felt. The report shows that by the late 1920s the company had not only acquired shares in businesses in Canada and the USA, but also had a controlling interest in French company La Compagnie Francaise du Linoleum Nairn and had set up Michael Nairn & Co (Australia).

Elsewhere in Fife, linoleum production provided work in Newburgh, through the Tayside Floorcloth Company and in Falkland, where once weavers had spun for Royal visitors, the textile mills evolved to produce linoleum and other floor coverings too.

But the successful production of linoleum in Fife didn't just benefit the county in economic terms by providing pay packets and jobs. Fife's well-known tradition of philanthropy shone through and those who were at the heart of the industry provided benefits to the community for generations to come through gifts of public parks such as Ravenscraig and Beveridge Park, which remain popular today, as well as art galleries, museums and libraries.

But if the communities were well provided for, so were the workers themselves. It is said that workers at Nairn's factories could consult company nurses and had the opportunity to join sports and social teams – with one other factory following the lead of many mining communities and forming its own brass band.

Like the mining industry in Fife, boom time for the linoleum industry was finite. Although the factories in Kirkcaldy remained strong throughout the Second World War, changing much of their work in support of the war effort and even producing casings for the 'earthquake bombs', the post-war era brought a dramatic decline.

Changing tastes and lifestyles saw linoleum becoming less popular and by the 1960s the linoleum industry in Fife had all but disappeared. Just one company remains in Kirkcaldy. Forbo Nairn, a descendant of the original Michael Nairn Company, is now owned by industry leading Swiss company Forbo.

While production might still continue, it's not enough to give rise to the distinctive smell that wafted over the town for many years – tickling the noses of all who passed through making sure that, just as the boy on the train exclaimed: 'I ken mysel' by the queer-like smell, that the next stop's Kirkcaddy!'. (Excerpt from The Boy on the Train, by Mary Campbell Smith, 1913.)

LOCAL BUSINESSES

KIRKCALDY

Accommodation

Strathern Hotel and Restaurant, 2 Wishart Place, Kirkcaldy, KY1 2AS. Tel 01592 652210, www.thestrathearnhotel.co.uk

Ahaven B&B, 288 High Street, Kirkcaldy, KY1 1LB. Tel: 01592 267779, www.ahaven.co.uk

Food and Beverage

Links Grocers, 137 Links Street, Kirkcaldy, KY1 1QR. Tel: 01592 206813

Good News, 113 Links Street, Kirkcaldy, KY1 1QL. Tel: 01592 206444

The Crafty Bite Café, 343 High Street, Kirkcaldy, KY1 1JN. Tel: 01592 200019 www.thecraftybite.co.uk

Golden Bite Café, 79 High Street, Kirkcaldy, KY1 1LL. Tel: 01592 590900

The Sandwich Shop, 409 High Street, Kirkcaldy, KY1 2SG. Tel: 01592 642266

La Speranza Café, 73 High Street, Kirkcaldy, KY1 1LL. Tel: 01592 263740

New York Sandwich Company, 465-467 High Street, Kirkcaldy, KY1 2SN. Tel: 01592 204200

The Exchequer Pub and Restaurant, 60-64 High Street, Kirkcaldy, KY1 1NB. Tel: 01592 646635 www.barracudagroup.co.uk/pubs/ exchequer.html

The Durbar Restaurant, 282-284 High Street, Kirkcaldy, KY1 1LB. Tel: 01592 265795

LOCAL BUSINESSES

KIRKCALDY

Food and Beverage (cont)

Glen Bakers, 266 Links Street, Kirkcaldy, KY1 1SG

Aveseo's Takeaway, 135 Links Street, Kirkcaldy, KY1 1QR. Tel: 01592 264123

Happy Valley Chinese Takeaway, 1 High Street, Kirkcaldy, KY1 1LQ. Tel: 01592 204504

New Maxim Restaurant, 3-5b High Street, Kirkcaldy, KY1 1LQ. Tel: 01592 204504

Stuarts the Bakers and Café, 25 High Street, Kirkcaldy, KY1 1LU. Tel: 01592 260831

L&A Valente Fish and Chips, 21 High Street, Kirkcaldy, KY1 1LQ. Tel: 01592 205744

The Penny Farthing Pub, 33-35 High Street, Kirkcaldy, KY1 1LL. Tel: 01592 263181

Tony's Kebabs, 59 High Street, Kirkcaldy, KY1 1LL. Tel: 01592 640555

Efes Kebabs, 51 High Street, Kirkcaldy, KY1 1LL. Tel: 01592 644809

Chicken Cottage, 80b High Street, Kirkcaldy, KY1 1NB. Tel: 01592 724395

Cafe Continental Bar and Restaurant, 6 Hill Place, Kirkcaldy, KY1 1BB. Tel: 01592 641811, www.cafecontinental.co.uk

The Harbour Bar, 473 High Street, Kirkcaldy, KY1 2SN. Tel: 01592 264270

The Path Tavern, 7 Mid Street, Kirkcaldy, KY1 2PE. Tel: 01592 263271 www.thapathtavern.co.uk

The Robert Nairn Bar and Restaurant, 2-6 Kirk Wynd, Kirkcaldy, KY1 1EH. Tel: 01592 205049, www.jdwetherspoon.co.uk/home/pubs/the-robert-nairn

Bar Itza Bar and Restaurant, 50 High Street, Kirkcaldy, KY1 1NA. Tel: 01592 204504, www.baritza.com

Betty Nichols Bar and Restaurant, 297 High Street, Kirkcaldy, KY1 1JL. Tel: 01592 642083 www.bettynicols.co.uk

The Chocolate Box, 7b High Street, Kirkcaldy. Tel: 01592 263996

News Plus, 55 High Street, Kirkcaldy. Tel: 01592 205786

Lidl, Gas Wynd Esplanade, Kirkcaldy, KY1 1SL. Tel: 0870 444 1234

Outdoor Clothing

Franks Army Stores, 14-15 Olympia Arcade, Kirkcaldy, KY1 1QF. Tel: 01592 591234 www.franksarmystores.com

Post Office

Premier Store, 221 Links Street, Kirkcaldy, KY1 1QS

Medical

Lloyds Pharmacy, 18 High Street, Kirkcaldy, KY1 1LU, Tel: 01592 269400

WEST WEMYSS

Food and Beverage

West Wemyss Walk Inn Café, 61-63 Main Street, West Wemyss, KY1 4SW. Tel: 01592 652001 www.westwemysscommunity.co.uk

LOCAL BUSINESSES

DYSART

Accommodation

The Royal Hotel, 20 Townshead, Dysart, KY1 2XQ. Tel: 01592 654112, www.royalhotelfife.co.uk

Merchant House B&B, 44 East Quality Street, Dysart, KY1 2TN. Tel: 01592 265917 www.merchanthouse.info

Food and Beverage

Carlton Bakers, 18 Cross Street, Dysart, KY1 2UE. Tel: 01592 651577

The Harbour Bistro, Hot Pot Wynd, Dysart, KY1 2TQ. Tel: 01592 654862 www.theharbourmastershouse.co.uk

Man I Rock Pub, 101 High Street, Dysart, KY1 2UL. Tel: 01592 651944, www.man-i-the-rock.piczo.com

The Cross Takeaway, 30 Cross Street, Dysart, KY1 2UE. Tel: 01592 654595

Tower Stores, 46 High Street, Dysart, KY1 2UG. Tel: 01592 651288

J.A Glass, Whisky Merchants, 9-11 High Street, Dysart, KY1 2 UG. Tel: 01592 651850 www.jaglass.co.uk

Post Office

Dysart Post Office and General Store, 50 High Street, Dysart, KY1 2UG. Tel: 01592 651528

Medical

Dysart Pharmacy, 21 HighStreet, Dysart, KY12UG. www.pharmacycentre.com

Tourist Attraction

Coastal Centre, Harbourmasters House, Hot Pot Wynd, Dysart, KY1 2TQ, Tel: 01592 656080, www. fifecoastalpath.co.uk

Leven

P

04 🏊

Lower Methil
Heritage Centre °

Methil Docks

A955

A915

Buckhaven

Methil

• Buckhaven Museum

03
02

• Macduff's Castle
P • Wemyss Caves

East Wemyss

A955

• Wemyss Castle

P 01

Welcome Port 🦆

01   **West Wemyss Walk Inn**
     61-63 Main Street KY1 4SW

02   **The Railway Tavern**
     24 Lawrance Street KY8 1BQ

03   **Burts Bar**
     44 Randolph Street KY8 1AT

04   **Levenmouth Swimming Pool**
     Promenade KY8 4PA

Fife Coastal Path **Distances**

West Wemyss to Leven Links
6.9 km / 4.3 miles

West Wemyss to Leven Links

CHAPTER NINE

WEST WEMYSS TO LEVEN LINKS

THIS section of the Fife Coastal Path starting at the Harbour Car Park is 6.5 miles long (10.4 km) and takes in the quaint Wemyss villages, historic castles and the modern towns of Buckhaven, Methil and Leven.

West Wemyss used to be one of the most important ports in Fife, with sailing ships coming from all over the Continent to trade coal and salt. The harbour dates from the 16th century and one of the earliest records was of a ship docking from London carrying cloths and a few rats which came ashore and brought the plague to Fife, devastating the population.

It may be hard to imagine that now because the harbour is so small. However, the existing harbour is only the outer harbour, the main harbour was filled in and grassed over. The village has declined with the mining industry. In the middle of the village and worth a look, is the 16th century Tolbooth with its clock steeple and prison cell.

At the end of the main street is St Adrian's Church, named after a 9th century saint. It was built in 1890 as the parish church for West Wemyss. The graveyard is older than the church itself. After the church, the path goes below Wemyss Castle dating from the 14th century (although altered many times since). In the rocks to the west of the Castle is Green Jean's Cave, now bricked up and named after the Castle's mythical ghost! I don't believe in ghosts, but even if I did, with a name like Green Jean, I certainly wouldn't want to meet her.

The path now skirts some woodland where wood anemone, lesser celandine and primrose carpet the ground in spring. It then crosses the reclaimed land on the site of the Michael Colliery, which closed in 1967 after a fire killed nine men. To the east of the village the path reaches the famous Wemyss Caves. In most of these caves are Pictish markings made between AD500 and 900. There are more markings in these caves than all the others in Britain put together.

The path now climbs up to Macduff Castle, believed to be connected to the Thane of Fife, slayer of the Scottish king Macbeth. The building that remains today is dated after that time and was the one that was burnt on the orders of Edward I. Growing in this area is alexanders, a plant used as a vegetable that is often found in association with castles.

The path now follows the line of an old railway into Buckhaven. It was from here that I got my first sighting of one of Fife's sea eagles. These birds were extinct in Britain by the early 20th century, sadly due mainly to illegal killing.

There has been a successful reintroduction programme on the west coast of

Macduff Castle, above, dates back to the time of Macbeth and below, Wemyss Caves where Pictish markings made between AD500 and 900 can be seen

Scotland, and now they have been reintroduced in Fife to try to re-establish an eastern population. Of course, I can't tell you that you will see one here, or on any other part of the Path, they are quite unpredictable. But you might get lucky somewhere along the way.

Many local birdwatchers are keen to get a sighting of one, but are not sure if they will be able to tell the difference between a sea eagle and one of the many buzzards that live in Fife. I always tell them that when they see one they will know for sure...simply because of the difference in size. The sea eagle is Britain's biggest bird of prey and has been nicknamed 'the flying barn door'. As a rule of thumb, if you look up and think 'is that a sea eagle?', then the answer is no. If, however, you look up and think 'crikey look at the size of that bird', then you have most probably been lucky enough to spot a sea eagle.

Buckhaven was once a prosperous fishing village – in the 19th century it had the second largest fleet in Scotland. Now, the harbour is disused and most of the fishermen's cottages gone. A display on the town's history can be seen in the local museum. Methil is now a modern industrial town making a living from its docks, fabrication yard and the power station. However, there was a thriving salt and coal industry in the area. Coal exporting was such a success that at its peak, almost 20,000 people lived in Methil. The towns of Methil and Leven are joined by the Bawbee Bridge (a bawbee was a Scottish halfpenny and that's how much you paid for the toll to cross the original bridge). The expanse of Largo Bay can be seen from Leven Promenade and is an excellent area to watch birds in the winter.

Did You Know?
Coal industry

No matter where you go in Fife, you'll never be far from a site marking part of Fife's most significant industrial legacy – mining.

Fife was once known as the powerhouse of Scotland, with the heaviest concentration of mines in the country, particularly around the Kirkcaldy area, but also boasted one of the most modern mines in the country too. But this pride in our industrial past is coupled with the burden of the darker side of mining: poor conditions, child labour and mining disasters that left their mark in Fife for decades to come.

Fife's mining history stretches much further back into the reaches of time that might be imagined. Although records first record that mining was taking place in Pittencrieff Glen in the late 13th century it is thought likely that mining was already underway in various parts of the county well before this date.

Seams of coal running under Fife led to the development of pits broadly categorised into East, West or Central Fife. And from the earliest days of mining coal was always in high demand, with another major Fife industry, salt production, providing much of the earliest demand along the coastline. One of the best known sites of salt production was that of Preston Island on the Forth Estuary where land owner Sir Robert Preston constructed a coal mine to provide the fire to evaporate water from large pans – leaving just the salt to be harvested.

By the mid-19th century demand for coal was so high that Fife's industry was flourishing with significant numbers of pits – up to 50 at one point – being sunk in the area. Harbours in West Wemyss, Charleston and St David's expanded to meet the export demands and 'new' ones in coastal towns such as Burntisland and Methil also emerged to keep up with the volume of coal being produced.

During such industrious times it is unsurprising that Fife's coal mines came to be dominated by three major forces: the Fife Coal Company; Lochgelly Iron and Coal Company and the Wemyss Coal Company. These three shaped and directed the majority of Fife's coal production with the Fife Coal Company being, at one point, the largest coal company in Scotland and dominating the market with the most modern pit in the country, at Comrie.

The industry reached its peak in 1913 when a staggering 9.5 million tonnes was produced. However success was limited as the start of World War I marked an end of exports and a decline in demand for coal from which Fife's coal industry was never to fully recover.

The long mining history in Fife was, however, also marked by the price paid by local people and communities for this dangerous and dirty profession. In 1842 the Children's Employment Commission found that mining conditions in Fife were among the worst in Britain and, as a direct result, children under the age of 10 were banned from working underground. Statistical records from 1838 give some perspective stating: 'The Wemyss coal-pit employs 140 men, 24 boys and 42 girls.' But while working underground might no longer be permitted, women and children were still heavily employed, undertaking duties such as sorting coal at the pithead.

Despite vast improvements in conditions for workers and engineering advances, mining remained a dangerous occupation for all involved. The date of October 28, 1939 remains one of the bleakest days in Fife's mining history when 35 men lost their lives in an explosion in the Valleyfield mine, in West Fife. A memorial to the dead stands on the site of the colliery in Valleyfield and the Valleyfield Disaster Memorial also stands in the town. The Carnegie Library in Dunfermline also holds the Fife Mining Memorial Book, which lists all those who lost their lives in pits in the county.

Although opencast mining continues in Fife to this day, there are no longer

At one time Fife had more working coal pits than anywhere else in Scotland

any deep mines in operation in Fife. Closures began to take place during the mid-1960s, but it was the 1980s that saw the decimation of the mining industry in Fife.

Although Fife had more working pits than anywhere else in Scotland at the start of the 1980s, by the end of the decade a programme of closures and the effect of the miners' strike had taken its toll and almost all were closed, with mass redundancies devastating communities across Fife.

The last deep mine, at Longannet, closed in 2002 marking the end of a remarkable era in Fife's history.

LOCAL BUSINESSES

EAST WEMYSS

Food and Beverage

Costcutter Convenience Store, 17 Main Street, East Wemyss, KY1 4RE. Tel: 01592 715824

Tourist Attraction

Wemyss Caves, East Wemyss, www. wemysscaves.co.uk

LOCAL BUSINESSES

BUCKHAVEN

Food and Beverage

The Railway Tavern, 24 Lawrence Street, Buckhaven, KY8 1BQ. Tel: 01592 713243

Burts Bar, 44 Randolph Street, Buckhaven, KY8 1AT (Welcome Port)

Full House Takeway, 65 College Street, Buckhaven, KY8 1JY. Tel: 01592 713278

Robbie's Rolls Takeaway, 24 College Street, Buckhaven, KY8 1JX

Stuarts Bakers, 10-12 College Street, Buckhaven, KY8 1JX. Tel: 01592 714199

Stuarts Bakers, 100-102 Wellesley Road, Buckhaven, KY8 1HT. Tel: 01592 712458

Post Office

Buckhaven Post Office, 106 Wellesley Road, Buckhaven, KY8 1HT. Tel: 01592 713440

METHIL

Food and Beverage

The Wellesley Inn, 683-685 Wellesley Road, Methil, KY8 3PQ. Tel: 01592 712600

Caspian Takeaway, 538 Wellesley Road, Methil, KY8 3PE. Tel: 01592 715242

Empire Bar, 413 High Street, Methil, KY8 3QP. Tel: 01333 425060

Salt 'N' Sauce Takeaway, 348 High Street, Methil, KY8 3EJ. Tel: 01333 424941

Ramzan Food Store, 206 High Street, Methil, KY8 3EF. Tel: 01333 439431

Cooks Café, 239 High Street, Methil, KY8 3ED. Tel: 01333 426325

East Dock Bar, 240-242 High Street, Methil, KY8 3EQ. Tel: 01333 426325

Post Office

Methil Post Office, 220 High Street, Methil, KY8 3EF. Tel: 0845 7223344

Medical

Alliance Pharmacy, 264 High Street, Methil, KY8 3EQ, Tel: 01333 423276

Tourist Attractions

Methil Heritage Centre, 272 High Street, Methil, KY8 3EQ. Tel: 01333 659339 www.methilheritage.org.uk

LEVEN

Accommodation

Dunclutha Guest House, 16 Victoria Road, Leven. Tel: 01333 425515, www.dunclutha.myby.co.uk

Caledonian Hotel and Restaurant, 81 High Street, Leven, KY8 4NG. Tel: 01333 424101 www.thecaledonianhotel-leven.co.uk

Lomond Guest House, 6 Church Road, Leven, KY8 4JE. Tel: 01333 300511, www.lomondguesthouse.co.uk

St Andrews Hall B&B, 4 Foreman Road, Leven, KY8 4HH. Tel: 0844 5449985, www.standrews-bb.co.uk

Food and Beverage

Sainsbury's Supermarket, Riverside Road, Leven, KY8 4LQ. Tel: 01333 439628

Cafe Inspire, Levenmouth Swimming Pool, Leven, KY8 4PA. Tel: 01333 695325, www.fifeleisure.org.uk

BBQ King, 3 Oswald Place, Leven, KY8 4NW. Tel: 01333 421064

LOCAL BUSINESSES

LEVEN

Food and Beverage (cont)

Shorehead Café, 3 Shorehead, Leven, KY8 4NR. Tel: 01333 428244

Real Spice, 11 Shorehead, Leven, KY8 4NR. Tel: 01333 422533

Greetings Newsagent, 4 High Street, Leven, KY8 4LZ. Tel: 01333 427439

RT Stuart Bakers, 37-39 High Street, Leven, KY8 4NE. Tel: 01333 429515

Bayne's Bakers, 51 High Street, Leven, KY8 4NE. Tel: 01333 429444

Cafe Rococo, 74 High Street, Leven, KY8 4NB. Tel: 07983 547383

Greggs Bakers, 53-55 High Street, Leven, KY8 4NE. Tel: 01333 422200

Leven Bay Café, 2 South Street, Leven, KY8 4NU. Tel: 01333 426383

Lidl, Mitchell Street, Leven, KY8 4HJ. Tel: 0870 444 1234

Blacketyside Farm Shop, Leven Road, Leven, KY8 5PX. Tel: 01333 423034

Tourist Attractions

Levenmouth Swimming Pool, Promenade, Leven, KY8 4PA. Tel: 01334 659325, www.fifeleisure.org.uk

Leven Links to Lower Largo

Lower Largo

Alexander
Selkirk
Memorial

04

03

Lundin Links

02

01

Largo Bay

Leven Links
Holiday Park

A915

A3

Welcome Port

01 **The Old Manor**
    55 Leven Road KY8 6AJ

02 **Lundin Links Hotel**
    Leven Road KY8 6AP

03 **Crusoe Hotel**
    2 Main Street   KY8 6BT

04 **Very Crafty**
    91 Main Street KY8 6BJ

Fife Coastal Path Distances

Leven Links to Lower Largo
3.2 km / 2 miles

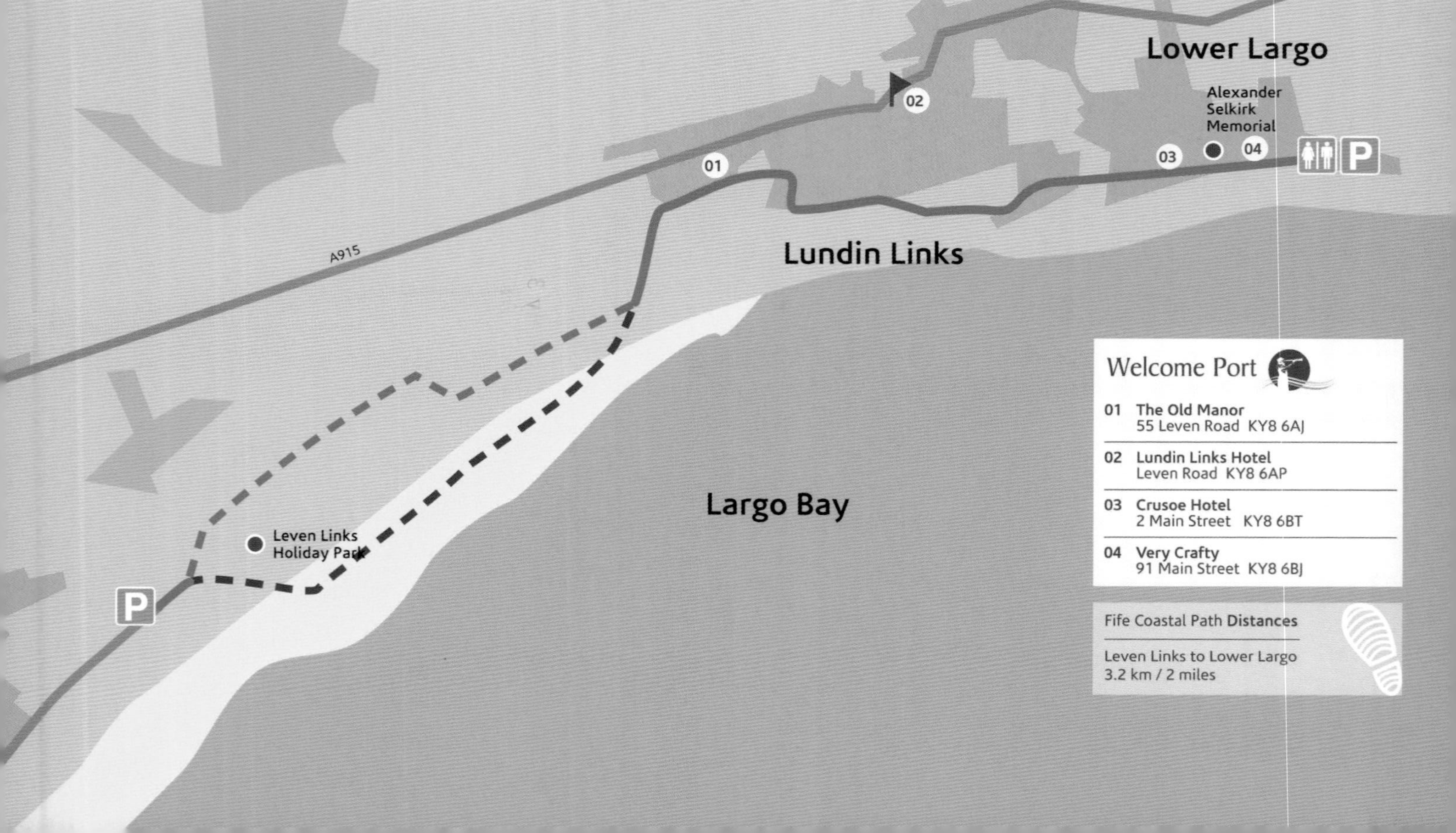

CHAPTER TEN

LEVEN LINKS TO LOWER LARGO

I HAVE been privileged to work as a Coastal Path Ranger for the past 15 years. I originally pursued this career because I have always loved wildlife and wild, open spaces. I felt that by becoming a Ranger I could help others to discover, enjoy and value the natural treasures around them – ultimately to the benefit of all.

The area I cover is Leven to St Andrews. Here, the Coastal Path crosses a varied and beautiful landscape. The route passes through towns and villages, which are full of history and interest, and follows a coastline rich in geology and wildlife.

However, if I had to pick a favourite section, it would have to be Shell Bay to Elie. This climbs over the headland of Kincraig and offers truly spectacular views of the surrounding landscape. There is wildlife interest too; in summer wild flowers include rockrose, viper's bugloss and greater knapweed and in winter you may spot wintering sea ducks. Grey seals often haul out on rocky islands off shore and you can sometimes hear their haunting and eerie calls – which add to the atmosphere of this stunning walk.

Countryside Ranger
Deirdre Munro

This section of the path is approximately 3 miles (4.8km) in length. The walking is level and for most of the way follows the sandy shoreline of the outstanding Largo Bay.

It begins at the car park to the west of Leven Links Caravan Park. The main route follows the beach that is sandy and level for most of its length, (though where the sand is soft and deep, walking may prove to be harder work).

It is worth keeping a look out for wildlife whatever the time of year. In winter this beach is a favourite haunt of sanderlings.

These little grey and white waders are a joy to watch as they run around at the water's edge picking up tasty morsels before retreating each time a wave comes in. Then there are other shorebirds to look out for including oystercatchers, curlews and ringed plovers.

Some of these birds are fairly easy to spot as they feed or rest along the shore. Oystercatchers are particularly distinctive with their smart black and white

Largo Bay is a favourite haunt of sanderlings in winter

plumage and carrot coloured bills. However with some of the smaller shore birds, you really need to 'get your eye in'.

At first glance, sanderling might easily be mistaken for little flecks of foam left by the waves as they move in and out. The similar sized ringed plovers are even harder to spot. Their plumage blends in perfectly with the pebbles and boulders that are strewn along the beach. There is even more to see if you look a little bit further out from the shore.

Eider ducks can often be seen out at sea and terns and gannets dive off shore during the summer months. Toward the eastern end of the beach, protruding rocks are popular sites for harbour seals. These often rest with their head and tail turned upwards as they inquisitively watch the comings and goings on the beach.

This sometimes gives them the characteristic outline of an upturned banana, particularly when viewed from a distance. The harbour or common seal is one of two species of seal that can be found along the Fife shore. The other is the larger, more 'roman nosed' grey.

This part of Largo Bay is also where I enjoyed my best sighting of bottlenose dolphins. One day a large group of these fascinating animals were passing surprisingly close to the shore. They moved at speed, often breaching clear of the water, and all who saw them were treated to a wonderful display of power and grace.

You might even be lucky enough to spot a pod of dolphins in Largo Bay

It was a warm afternoon in late summer and there was quite a few walkers scattered along the beach. When I looked back along the shore, I noticed that every one of them had stopped what they were doing and stood, utterly transfixed, watching the dolphins until they moved out of sight on their journey up the Forth.

At high tide, an alternative route follows a grassy path around the caravan park's northern boundary before continuing through the sand dunes that lie between the golf course and the beach. Both routes continue this way for just over a kilometre before converging and crossing the golf course at a point marked by timber posts. Please be alert here and pay attention to what golfers are doing and the direction in which they are playing. If in doubt it is safest to wait until they have played their shot.

The route then continues east, past the golf club house and on through the peaceful village of Lundin Links. Part of this stretch runs through the Massney Braes area, and this site is a particular favourite of mine, especially in spring and summer. It consists of a mixture of woodland, scrub, wild flowers and sand dunes. A network of smaller paths wind their way through scattered thickets of burnet rose and bramble, which in summer provide perfect cover for nesting birds, including whitethroat, wren, and song thrush.

The paths are lined with common and greater knapweed, red campion and rest harrow, all alive with the buzz and activity of numerous insects. Rabbits can

The view from Massney Braes - a real gem on the Fife Coastal Path

usually be seen here and are surprisingly tame, given that the area is popular with dog walkers.

The area borders a sheltered part of the coast, which like much of Largo Bay, is sandy and interspersed with rocks. Here shore birds can often be seen, particularly in winter, whilst in summer the quiet sheltered waters provide an ideal nursery for crèches of eider ducklings.

For anyone who treasures the sights and sounds of wildlife, I would urge you to pause here, perhaps rest on a bench or a handy rock and just take a few moments to watch and listen. Massney Braes is not a large area, nor is it a particularly well-known wildlife site or nature reserve, but to me, it is one of the real gems of the coastal path.

Lundin Links dates from the mid 19th century and is separated from Lower Largo by the Keil Burn that is crossed just downstream from the old railway viaduct where the river enters the sea by the harbour.

LOCAL BUSINESSES

LUNDIN LINKS

Accommodation

Old Manor Hotel and Restaurant, 55 Leven Road, Lundin Links. KY8 6AJ, Tel: 01333 320868
www.theoldmanorhotel.co.uk

Lundin Links Hotel and Restaurant, Leven Road, Lundin Links, KY8 6AP.
Tel: 01333 320327
www.lundin-links-hotel.co.uk

Hillhead House Holiday Rentals, 5 Hillend Street, Lundin Links.
Tel: 0784 3203717

Food and Beverage

Premier Store, 17 Leven Road, Lundin Links, KY8 6AQ. Tel: 01333 320360

RT Stuart Bakers, 7 Leven Road, Lundin Links, KY8 6AQ. Tel: 01333 320213

Post Office

Lundin Links Post Office, 17 Leven Road, Lundin Links, KY8 6AQ.
Tel: 01333 320360

LOWER LARGO

Accommodation

Crusoe Hotel and Restaurant, 2 Main Street, Lower Largo, KY8 6BT.
Tel: 01333 320759 www.crusoehotel.co.uk (Welcome Port)

Food and Beverage

The Railway Inn, 1 Station Wynd, Lower Largo, KY8 6BU. Tel: 01333 320329

Very Crafty Café, 91 Main Street, Lower Largo, KY8 6BJ. Tel: 01333 320006 (Welcome Port)

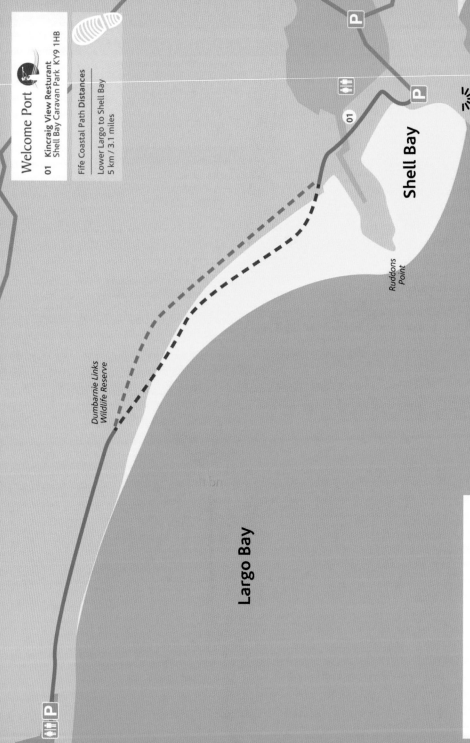

Welcome Port

01 **Kincraig View Resturant**
Shell Bay Caravan Park KY9 1HB

Fife Coastal Path Distances

Lower Largo to Shell Bay
5 km / 3.1 miles

**Dumbarnie Links
Wildlife Reserve**

Largo Bay

**Ruddons
Point**

Shell Bay

**Kincraig
Head**

Lower Largo to Shell Bay

CHAPTER ELEVEN

LOWER LARGO TO SHELL BAY

THIS section, which starts at Temple Car Park, is 4 miles in length (6.4 km) and finishes at Shell Bay Caravan Park. It consists of level walking initially following the line of the old railway and then descending onto the sandy shore. This is an invigorating walk, which offers spacious views and a rich variety of birdlife.

Lower Largo is perhaps best known as the birthplace of Alexander Selkirk. Born in 1676, he spent four years on an island in the South Pacific. His adventures there became the inspiration for Daniel Defoe's famous fictional character, Robinson Crusoe. You can read more about him at the end of this chapter.

His statue can be seen amongst the row of cottages to your left as you follow the route through narrow streets leading you to the Temple Car Park, which is signposted from the main coast road. Here there is an attractive landscaped area complete with picnic tables and information panels.

The name Temple may refer to the Knights Templar, dating back to the 12th century. The knights served to protect pilgrims on their way to St Andrews.

The route begins by climbing a flight of steps to join the line of the old coastal railway. This was closed in 1965, but in its day it must have provided rail passengers with some superb views of the adjacent coastline.

The bank on which the railway was built now provides us with an ideal surface for the Coastal Path. Follow this east, through two sets of kissing gates. The views soon open up as the trees, shrubs and the last houses of the village are left behind.

In late spring and summer the path here is bordered by a colourful display of wild flowers. Among them are purple milk vetch, rest harrow, lady's bedstraw, black and greater knapweed and field scabious. These in turn attract a host of insects. Bees and hoverflies fly busily from one blossom to another while a closer look at the foliage and flower heads may well reveal caterpillars and red soldier beetles. On warm summer days, you might see one of my favourite insects – the six spot burnet moth.

If you ask people what the difference is between a moth and a butterfly, most will tell you that moths fly at night and are generally dull brown whereas butterflies are brightly coloured and fly during day time. However, six spot burnet moths prove that this is not always the case! Fully active in daylight hours, they sport colours that rival any butterfly. The moth's name comes from the bright crimson spots that are backed by deep metallic green. A truly stunning little moth.

Above, bees enjoying the local Knapweed
and below, the World War II gun emplacements

Later, in the summer, look out for the caterpillars of another brightly coloured day flying moth, the cinnabar. These caterpillars feed on bright yellow ragwort flowers. Farmers and horse owners regard ragwort as a serious pest since the leaves contain a poison, which can harm livestock if consumed. However the cinnabar caterpillars use this to their own advantage.

As they feed on the plant, the poison is absorbed and stored in their skin – which then deters predators from eating them. To advertise this, the caterpillars are brightly coloured, each bearing striking orange and black stripes. This serves as a warning to any potential predator on the lookout for a meal – 'don't eat me – I'm poisonous!'

From late summer and autumn through winter, finches and other small birds gather in flocks to forage together. These winter flocks can often be seen in the surrounding fields as they restlessly fly from one area to another in search of seeds.

The route continues along the railway for approximately one kilometre, passing through a further kissing gate, until a bridge crosses a burn to where some timber steps lead down to a level area adjacent to the sand dunes.

From this point the path follows the coast rather than the old railway. Following the waymarkers, the Dumbarnie Wildlife Reserve is soon reached. Owned and managed by the Scottish Wildlife Trust, this is an excellent area for duneland flowers. An information panel is well worth reading and lets you know what to look out for.

Here there is also a high tide/low tide split in the path. The high tide route follows a path through the reserve, the centre of which forms a hollow, which can become flooded in winter. In this case a route can easily be picked along the higher ground to your right.

Two buildings are passed which date from World War II and served as gun emplacements. A line of concrete anti-tank blocks marks the reserve's eastern boundary and a rough, undulating path then continues through the dunes.

The low tide route simply follows the beach until both routes converge at the Cocklemill Burn, which joins the sea at the eastern end of Largo Bay.

Not far from Dumbarnie Wildlife Reserve some fencing marks the spot where coastal stabilisation work was carried out several years ago in an area which was badly affected by erosion. The project involved installing chestnut fences so that sand blown by the wind could build up around them. This allows coastal vegetation to become established, which in turn protects the land from further erosion.

Some of the fences are now almost completely buried beneath the accumulated sand with the result that grasses have successfully spread over the area. Information panels explain how this important work helps to protect the coastal environment.

Both the high and low tide routes offer wonderful views of the spacious, windswept landscape. The cries of shore birds add to the atmosphere and the uplifting song of the skylark can be heard above the dunes throughout spring and summer. Fence posts along the shore often serve as useful perches for handsome red and black stonechats.

Once the Cocklemill Burn is reached the route heads inland for a short distance before crossing the burn via two timber bridges. In spring and early summer sand martins nest along the high sandy banks of the Cocklemill.

Like their close relatives house martins and swallows, sand martins winter in Africa returning to our shores each year to breed. The vertical sand banks of the Cocklemill are perfect for them to excavate their nest tunnels.

If you are walking in this area at nesting time, it's a good idea to stop, sit down, perhaps take out a flask of tea or coffee, and quietly observe the birds for a while. Sand martins are superb, active flyers and it is great fun to watch their comings and goings around a nest colony. Continuing on your way, a band of conifer trees can be seen straight ahead. The path continues through a gap in the trees to where another line of anti-tank blocks marks the beginning of Shell Bay Caravan Park.

If you are a keen bird watcher it may be worth taking a short detour around Ruddon's Point, to your right. In winter, this offers an excellent sea watching point. Largo Bay supports large numbers of over wintering sea duck, which include long-tailed duck, common and velvet scoter and occasional sightings of the rarer surf scoter. Eiders are present all year.

Did You Know?
Alexander Selkirk

Readers of Daniel Defoe's classic, *Robinson Crusoe,* might be forgiven for thinking that the inspiration for the eponymous island castaway came from the author's imagination or from a traditional tale of life on the high seas. But the truth, being truly stranger than fiction, is that the much-loved hero is based on Fife seafarer, Alexander Selkirk.

Born in Lower Largo in 1676, Alexander Selkirk lived a colourful and controversial life, best remembered for the four-and-half-years he endured alone on the small and uninhabited island of Mas a Tierra, 400 miles off the Chilean coast.

Selkirk was the son of a tanner and shoemaker and his formative years in the Fife village were to set the tone for the rest of his life. Selkirk's temper was such that it made for difficult relationships with many who crossed his path; from

Statue of Alexander Selkirk-the inspiration for Daniel Defoe's classic *Robinson Crusoe*

members of his family to the Kirk session at his local church and later those who sailed with him.

But, it was a summons by the Lower Largo Kirk in 1695 – on the grounds of his behaviour in church – that led to him taking off to chance his luck at sea. Some records say he skipped town before the Kirk caught up with him, others suggest that duly chastised he took off to sea, but within a short time Selkirk was working as a privateer – the 'legitimate' form of piracy in its time.

As an able seaman Selkirk found work with well-known buccaneer, William Dampier and his colleague, Thomas Stradling and it was this that led to the fateful journey on the ship the Cinque Ports towards the end of 1704.

Under the command of Thomas Stradling, the Cinque Ports made its way towards the coast of South America having parted, acrimoniously, from William Dampier's ship St George. But while the ship dropped anchor in the Juan Fernandez archipelago, it became apparent that Selkirk's infamous temper was at work again – and to seal his fate as a castaway.

But what comes as the greatest surprise to most readers of Selkirk's tale is that rather than being forcibly removed to Mas a Tierra, he chose to be left there.

The condition of the Cinque Ports was such that it caused Selkirk a great deal of concern and justifiably so, as the crew later had to abandon ship with very few surviving. With the ship riddled with worms and short of sails, Alexander Selkirk used the time on Mas a Tierra to attempt to convince the crew to mutiny against Captain Stradling.

Though his attempts to gain the confidence of the crew failed, he remained true to his earlier form and stubbornly remained on the island alone. And it was here he was to remain with his seaman's chest – a gun, a knife, a hatchet, oats and tobacco, a Bible, and some navigational instruments – until his rescue in 1709.

Accounts of his time on the island could rival the best survival guides packing bookshelves all over the world today.

Selkirk used the feral goats as a source of nourishment, as well as seafood and crops that he cultivated from the native species on the island. He built huts for shelter using wood from the island's trees and made use of the skills he had learned from his tanner father to fashion clothes from the hides of the animals he had caught and eaten.

And while this tale of survival against the odds is surprising in itself, the mental state of Selkirk upon his rescue is perhaps the most startling – accounts of his return from solitude speak of his calm demeanour. Essayist Richard Steele wrote in 1713, after a series of interviews with Selkirk: 'There was a strong, but cheerful seriousness in his look and a certain disregard to the ordinary things about him, as if he had been sunk in thought. The man frequently bewailed his return to the world, which could not, he said, with all its enjoyments, restore him to the tranquillity of his solitude.'

LOCAL BUSINESSES

SHELL BAY

Accommodation

Elie Holiday Park, Shell Bay, KY9 1HB. Tel: 01333 330283, www.abbeyford. com/our-parks/elie-holiday-park

Scotland Holiday Home, Units A48, A46 and A44, Shell Bay, KY9 1HB. www.scotlandholidayhome.co.uk

Food and Beverage

Kincraig View Restaurant, Shell Bay, KY9 1HB. Tel: 01333 330283, www.abbeyford.com/our-parks/elie-holiday-park (Welcome Port)

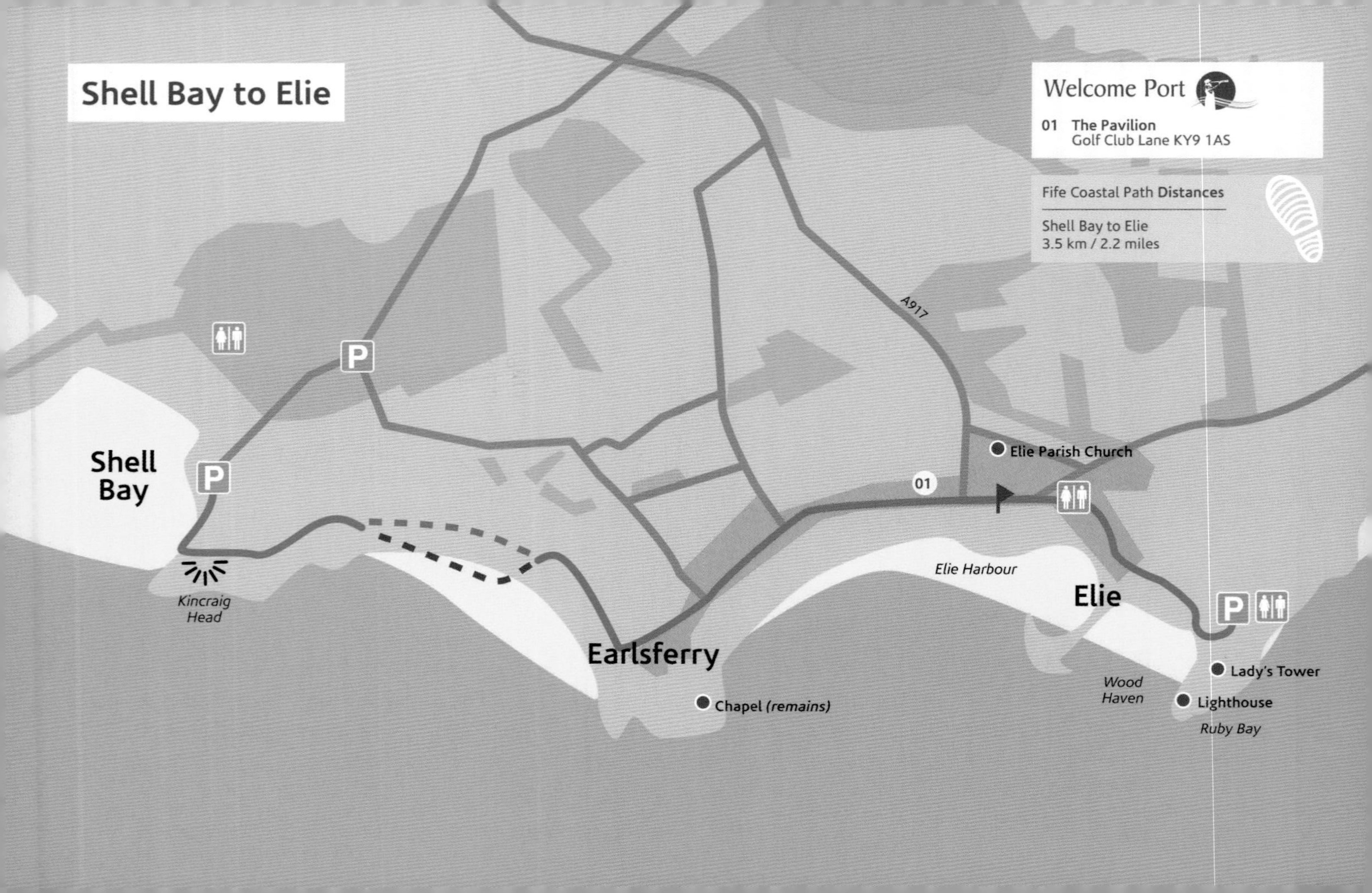

Shell Bay to Elie

Welcome Port

01 The Pavilion
Golf Club Lane KY9 1AS

Fife Coastal Path Distances

Shell Bay to Elie
3.5 km / 2.2 miles

A917

01

Elie Parish Church

Elie

Elie Harbour

Wood Haven

Ruby Bay

● Lady's Tower

● Lighthouse

Earlsferry

● Chapel (remains)

Kincraig Head

Shell Bay

P

CHAPTER TWELVE

SHELL BAY TO ELIE

THIS section is approximately 3 miles (4.8 km) in length and can be rough and muddy in places. It follows a narrow path over Kincraig and offers magnificent views over the Forth and beyond. The route is exposed in places and stout footwear is a must.

The well-named Shell Bay, with its golden sandy beach, lies between Ruddon's Point in the west and Kincraig to the east. The area is used as a caravan park that is busy in spring and summer, but closed between November and March.

If you are starting your walk at Shell Bay, you have a choice of car park. The main Coastal Path car park is free and is situated at the end of the main caravan park access road. From here there is a short walk, of approximately five minutes, to the coast.

You can also park on the shore, closer to the start of the walk, but this costs £1 per day. Tickets can be bought at the caravan park reception. Please be aware though, that in winter, the park gates close at 4pm, so your car will need to be out of the shore car park by then.

The route begins by crossing a small footbridge and following a narrow path which climbs at first, but soon becomes level as it heads east between arable fields to the left and the boulder-strewn shore to the right. Soon the path turns around the point and some stone steps are reached, which take you to a higher level.

The route continues as before until a further flight of steps takes you up again. What you are actually doing here is climbing a series of raised beaches, which perfectly illustrate the varying sea levels through the ages. The route continues over the top of Kincraig, taking you past a variety of concrete buildings. These are gun emplacements and lookouts, which date from WWII. From this point on the view must surely be one of the highlights of the whole Coastal Path experience.

To the west there is the wide sweep of Largo Bay, backed by the distinctive outline of Largo Law. To the east lie the golden sands of West Bay bordered by the Golf Course with the Royal Burghs of Earlsferry and Elie beyond. The slopes above the golf course are rich in botanical interest including rockrose, greater knapweed and viper's bugloss. It is well worth taking your camera along for this section. Indeed, this is where the superb cover photograph of Earlsferry Bay, looking over to Elie was taken.

Soon, the route follows a flight of stone steps down to the shore by the golf

The view across Shell Bay

course. Once down, timber steps lead from the dunes to the beach and the main route follows this to the eastern end. At high tide follow the path through the dunes.

The routes converge and cross the golf course at Sea Tangle Road, (please remember to pay close attention to any golf course

Who knows who you might meet on your travels along the Fife Coastal Path!

warning notices), before following a wide grassy path around the area known as Chapel Green. This is named after an 11th century chapel, which was used by pilgrims travelling to St Andrews. All that is left now is a ruined gable.

Follow the Coastal Path signs through Earlsferry and Elie. This area was also an important place for pilgrims. A ferry ran from North Berwick until the latth century, helping pilgrims to continue their journey to St Andrews. Legend says that Earlsferry was made a Royal Burgh and got its name because people from the tiny village transported Macduff, Earl of Fife over the Forth when he was escaping from Macbeth.

Although these communities were once two separate and distinct Royal Burghs, they were formally united in 1929 and now form one continuous settlement.

The picturesque Elie Beach

THE ELIE CHAINWALK

For most, the length and variety of the Fife Coastal Path makes it enjoyable, challenging and ultimately, rewarding. But for those who are looking for something a little out of the ordinary or more adrenalin-fuelled, the Elie Chain Walk could be just the thing. For the Chain Walk is just that – a scramble around the cliffs of Kincraig Point using chains and it's not for the faint-hearted.

Although just one-and-a-half miles long, the Chain Walk offers all the excitement of something ten times the length. Starting at Shell Bay to the west of Elie and heading east around Kincraig Point to the end at Earlsferry beach, those who tackle it will make their way around the pools, caves and cliffs of the coast with the help of eight chains attached to the rock and footholds along the way. The chains vary in length from 10 to 50 feet and are attached at differing angles – making the walk a combination of vertical and horizontal walking, climbing and scrambling along the coastline.

Tackling the first chain and stepping on to the first foothold is reputedly the most difficult – whichever end you start at – and often described as literally taking a step into the unknown.

But, once that step has been taken, the rewards are great. Apart from the adrenaline rush of tackling the chains themselves, the walk gives a unique view out to the Forth with the waves crashing spectacularly close by. There are a few caves to be explored and rock pools teaming with marine life will excite children brave enough to make the trek. And for many, the highlight of the walk is a chance to see at close quarters the unique and unusual formations of the rocks

The Elie Chain Walk is just that - and not for the faint-hearted!

around Kincraig Point – some of which are volcanic of similar geological nature to those of Arthur's Seat in Edinburgh and the Bass Rock. The Chain Walk gives you a chance to get up close and personal with the coast in a way unlikely to be experienced again.

As with all adrenaline-driven adventures, there is an element of danger to undertaking the Chain Walk and precautions are advised. Careful planning of when to undertake the Walk is the key to doing it safely, as the tide can come in quickly and leave those who have timed it badly stranded. Allow up to three hours to complete the Chain Walk with the best time to start out being shortly after high-tide, leaving the maximum length of time to enjoy the walk and all that it offers before the next high tide returns. Sensible footwear and clothing are also advised as the route can be particularly slippery and – this being the east of Scotland – the weather can change suddenly.

The history and origins of the Elie Chain Walk remain unknown, but locally it is thought to date from the early 20th century and to have been put in place by local fishermen. But whatever its tale, it has secured its place in the hearts of many looking for a challenge that is, quite literally, off the beaten track.

The Chain Walk is inspected twice yearly under the management of Fife Council. Those who choose to use the Chain Walk should pay careful attention to the warning signs and be confident of their ability to undertake this unique experience.

LOCAL BUSINESSES

EARLSFERRY/ELIE

Accommodation

East Neuk Self Catering, The Park, Bank Street, Elie. Tel: 01333 330 219, www.elielet.com

Wadeslea House B&B, Wadeslea, Elie. Tel: 01333 330 942, www.eliebedandbreakfast.co.uk

Bed and Breakfast Elie, 1 High Street, Elie. Tel: 01333 331 157, www.bedandbreakfastelie.co.uk

East Coast Lets, Various Properties, Elie. Tel: 07970140183, www.eastcoastlets.com

Food and Beverage

The Golf Tavern, 5 Links Road, Earlsferry, KY9 1AW. Tel: 01333 330 610, www.golftavern-elie.com

The Pavillion Café, Golf Club Lane, Elie, KY9 1AS. Tel: 01333 331132, www.thepav.co.uk (Welcome Port)

Newsagent, 50 High Street, Elie, KY9 1DB. Tel: 01333 330213, elienewsagents@tiscali.co.uk

Elie Deli, 55 High Street, Elie, KY9 1BZ. Tel:01333 330323, www.eliedeli.co.uk

The Ship Inn, The Toft, Elie, KY9 1DT. Tel: 01333 330246, www.ship-elie.com

The Galley Takeaway, Elie Harbour, Elie, KY9 1DH. Tel: 01333 331145, www.eesc.org.uk

Banking

ATM, High Street, Elie, KY9 1BP

Elie to Anstruther

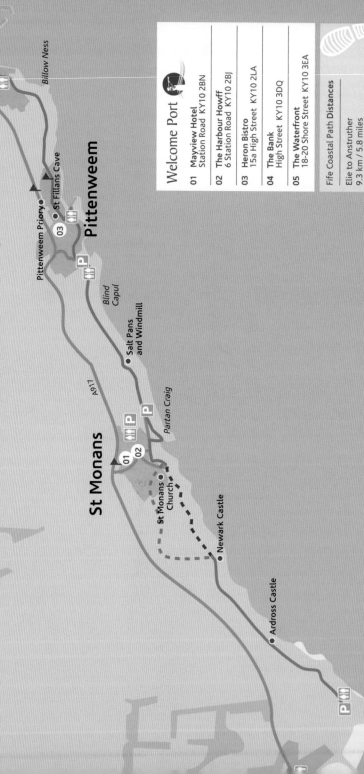

Welcome Port

01	**Mayview Hotel** Station Road KY10 2BN
02	**The Harbour Howff** 6 Station Road KY10 2BJ
03	**Heron Bistro** 15a High Street KY10 2LA
04	**The Bank** High Street KY10 3DQ
05	**The Waterfront** 18-20 Shore Street KY10 3EA

Fife Coastal Path Distances

Elie to Anstruther
9.3 km / 5.8 miles

Anstruther

Billow Ness

Pittenweem

St Fillans Cave

Pittenweem Priory

Blind Capul

Salt Pans and Windmill

A917

St Monans

Partan Craig

St Monans Church

Newark Castle

Ardross Castle

Lady's Tower

Lighthouse

Ruby Bay

CHAPTER THIRTEEN

ELIE TO ANSTRUTHER

THIS section is around 6.5 miles in length (10.4 km) and can be rough underfoot. It is full of geological, historical and wildlife interest, but it also includes several short sections of stone steps that may be uneven or slippy and take you through quaint little fishing villages. Stout footwear is essential, particularly in winter.

The official starting point for this section is Ruby Bay Car Park, Elie which is signposted from the main road. Ruby Bay gets its name from the clear red garnet called Elie rubies, which were once commonly found in this area. You may still be lucky enough to find a piece, so a wander along the beach, particularly the black volcanic sands around the lighthouse and Lady Tower may be well worthwhile.

The Coastal Path runs through the grassy area known as Shepherd's Knowe. In spring and early summer this area is transformed by a colourful display of wildflowers such as cowslips, black knapweed and birdsfoot trefoil, with thrift and white campion closer to the shore. Look out for small birds such as linnet, meadow pipit, stonechat and skylark. A short detour takes you to Elie Lighthouse, built in 1908 and Lady Tower, which was built around 1760 for Lady Janet Anstruther to use as a summerhouse.

There are good views from inside the tower and good photo opportunities. There is also a small bathing hut on the beach below the tower. Lady Anstruther apparently loved to bathe here and each time she did, she had a servant walk through Elie ringing a bell so that locals were warned to stay away.

Soon the route narrows and continues between the shore and the fields inland. After a while you reach the jumbled ruin of Ardross Castle. This was built around 1370 out of local sandstone. The path becomes slightly rougher and more undulating from here until another castle is reached. This is Newark Castle, built in the 15th century for the Sandilands Family.

Close by is a 16th century 'beehive doocot' originally built to keep pigeons as a valuable source of winter food. From this point to St Monans there is another high tide diversion, running along a field edge, before crossing a small bridge and rejoining the low tide route, near St Monans Church. This historical parish church was built in the 14th century by order of David II.

St Monans has been a small fishing village since the 14th century and today is a typical East Neuk village with its narrow streets of stone houses and its stone-built harbour.

Continuing along the path we reach the eastern end of the village where there are two car parks. One is situated towards the end of Forth Street, adjacent to

The windmill at St Monans, above, has been restored and is well worth a visit and below, is a meadow pipit enjoying the sunshine

the village common and has toilet facilities, which are usually open. The other is located along Rose Street. It is very small, but is recommended for users with mobility problems that would prevent them having to descend steps.

From either car park follow the signs to St Monans Windmill. This first part of the path is wide, level and suitable for most types of user. The windmill is set on a raised beach, above the site of a number of 18th century saltpans.

The salt industry made use of the coal that could not be sold commercially to heat saltwater in these pans. Salt production was a major industry all along the Fife coast. Sadly, the salt industry declined rapidly from 1830 when the tax on English salt was removed.

The windmill has been recently restored and is well worth a visit. There are useful information panels around the site. From here, the path continues east and becomes rougher and narrower. Look out for birds along the rocky shore such as redshank, oystercatcher or curlew. There is also interesting geology.

Midway between St Monans and Pittenweem, an interesting chunk of limestone sticks out from the shore. White with a ginger-coloured band, it bears the marks of a fossilised coral bed. Out to sea there are views of Berwick Law, Bass Rock and the Isle of May. This is a short section and the West Braes area of Pittenweem is soon reached. Here you can see an old bathing area and pool, which date back to before World War I.

The pool and the surroundings are a haven for all sorts of inter-tidal wildlife. If the tide is out and always be aware of what the tides are doing, this is a great area for a rock pool 'guddle'. This is an activity that is enjoyable for young and old alike.

Among the rocks and seaweed lives a truly fascinating array of creatures. Here you can find delights such as shore crabs, prawns, starfish, periwinkles, sea anemones, dog whelks, limpets, blennies and many, many more. The lives of these creatures are shaped by the endless cycle of the tides and they are beautifully adapted to cope with their coastal environment.

Whenever I take families or school groups to a rocky shore I always find that the adults invariably become every bit as engrossed as the children. There is always something of interest to be found in a rock pool.

One of my favourite rock pool inhabitants is the hermit crab. These little crabs have soft bodies and in order to protect themselves, they live in empty periwinkle or whelk shells, seeking out larger replacements as they grow. These are bold little creatures and if you watch a rock pool quietly for any length of time they will usually come out of hiding and continue to scurry about on their own business, which sometimes includes trying to pull a rival crab out of a particularly desirable shell!

Of course, you should always remember to treat rock pool creatures gently, and try to replace any rocks or stones just as you found them. Finally, don't think rock pool 'guddling' is just for children. As I said before adults get engrossed too and I'm sure you will enjoy it whatever your age.

Continuing through the attractive fishing village of Pittenweem, be sure to have a look at The Gyles and St Fillan's Cave, believed to be the place where St Fillan lived whilst converting the Picts to Christianity in the 7th century. The name Pittenweem is Pictish in origin and actually means 'town of the cave'. Follow the signs to the east end of Pittenweem and travel along a field edge for a short distance before turning right to descend a flight of stone steps leading to the coastline below.

This section follows the rocky shore of Billowness along the edge of Anstruther Golf Course which is the haunt of birds such as eider duck, turnstone, and shag. You may also spot grey seals as they watch you from the safety of the water. The path enters Anstruther near the Golf Club House.

St Fillan's Cave in the attractive fishing village of Pittenweem

Did You Know?
Islands of the Forth – East Neuk

There are many reasons why Fife's coastline is an enduringly popular place to enjoy the great outdoors. Visitors are drawn back to enjoy everything from the varied wildlife and nature to the pretty coastal towns, but the spectacular, ever-changing view offered across the Forth is undoubtedly one of the biggest pulls.

On the clearest days it seems almost possible to reach out and touch some of Edinburgh's most famous landmarks and even on the worst days it can be exhilarating to watch the weather rolling in from the sea. Whatever the weather, the islands that dot the Firth of Forth remain fascinating, each with their own unique qualities and tales to tell.

One of the most iconic islands, which can be seen from the East Fife coastline, is Bass Rock. This volcanic magma chamber plug is now recognised as a Site of Special Scientific Interest (SSSI) because of the gannet colony which nests there, but also has a fascinating history involving Royal visits, prisoners and classic literature.

The first inhabitant on the island is said to have been Baldred, a monk from the Lindisfarne monastery who was sent north to preach Christianity and stayed on the island in around the 8th century. By the 1400s Bass Rock was in the ownership of the Lauder family who built a castle on the island, one that they occupied continuously for many generations.

Such was the safety of Bass Rock that in the early 1400s King Robert III sent his threatened son James there to ensure his safe flight to Europe could be arranged. But, just as the island's remote nature ensured inhabitants could be kept safe it also ensured they could be kept there – against their will. The Bass Rock gained notoriety during the 15th century when James I used it as a political prison and this continued into the 17th century following Oliver Cromwell's invasion when the island fell out of the hands of the Lauders and became a prison for religious and political prisoners.

Famous Edinburgh novelist Robert Louis Stevenson drew on his knowledge and personal experiences of Bass Rock in writing *Catriona*, a sequel to his classic *Kidnapped*. Set in the times of the Jacobite Risings, the fate of the chief protagonist was sealed when he is imprisoned on the island.

Stevenson's knowledge of the island was gained through childhood experience – travelling from his home in Edinburgh to holiday in North Berwick. It is also claimed that his family was uniquely connected with the lighthouse on the island with some sources stating that his grandfather designed it.

Nowadays however, Bass Rock is less well known for its conflicts and turbulent times, but has gained a reputation as the world's biggest single island gannet colony with more than 150,000 gannets nesting here between February and October.

This spectacular bird now predominates on the island and those who make boat trips out to Bass Rock have the chance to view the famous 'dive-bombing' of these birds who can achieve speeds nearing 100 kilometres an hour as they enter the water, giving them the ability to catch fish out of the reach of most other birds.

For the less intrepid, the Scottish Seabird Centre has webcams installed on the island through which wildlife lovers from all over the world can view these beautiful birds.

The seabird centre also has webcams viewing the nearby, but lesser-known, island of Craigleith.

This tiny island is home to guillemots, cormorants, shags and puffins, thanks largely to a project called SOS Puffin which aimed to encourage puffins to return to the island by reinstating habitats which had been destroyed by an invasive plant, the tree mallow. The project is enjoying considerable success and volunteers continue to battle the tree mallow – winning a slow, but worthwhile battle.

On the opposite side of the Forth wildlife enthusiasts will also be held in thrall by the Isle of May. This tiny island, most easily accessed by boat from Anstruther, is home to an array of wildlife including what is thought to be the largest seal colony on the east coast. Up to 2,000 seal pups are thought to be in the area over the winter months. For a very lucky few, sightings around the Isle of May have also included dolphins and whales.

LOCAL BUSINESSES

ST MONAN'S

Accommodation

Mayview Hotel and Restaurant, 40 Station Road, St Monans, KY10 2BN
Tel: 01333 730564,
www.mayviewhotel.co.uk

Post Office

8 West Shore, St. Monans, KY10 2BS.
Tel: 01333 730240

PITTENWEEM

Accommodation

Albert Cottage B&B, 15 Viewforth Place, Pittenweem, KY10 2PZ.
Tel: 01333 313973,
www.albertcottagefife.co.uk

Rooms @ 25 B&B, 25 Charles Street, Pittenweem, KY10 2QH.
Tel: 01333 313306,
www.roomsat25.co.uk

Fife Coastal Path Holidays, 2 Glebe Park, Pittenweem, KY 102 NA.
Tel: 01333 311184. info@
walkingfifecoastalpath.com
www.walkingfifecoastalpath.com

Food and Beverage

Traquair's Village Shop, 5 Market Place, Pittenweem, KY10 2PH.
Tel: 01333 311498

A J Nicolson Store, 17 Mid Shore, Pittenweem. Tel: 01333 310812

Heron Bistro, 15a High Street, Pittenweem. Tel: 01333 311014,
www.pittenweem-fife.co.uk

Fish and Chip Shop, 5 High Street, Pittenweem, KY10 2PZ.
Tel: 01333 311258

Pittenweem Inn and Restaurant, 42 Charles Street, Pittenweem, KY10 2QJ. Tel: 01333 311326, www. pittenweeminn.co.uk

The Larachmhor Tavern, 6 Midshore, Pittenweem, KY10 2NL.
Tel. 01333 311200

Medical

Pittenweem Pharmacy, Newsagent and Post Office, 7 Market Place, Pittenweem, KY10 2PH. Tel: 01333 311243

Galleries and Gift Shops

The Blue Door Gallery, South Loan, Pittenweem, KY10 2QN.
Tel: 01333 311254,

Fisher Studio and Gallery, 11-13 High Street, Pittenweem, KY10 2LA.
Tel: 01333 312255,
www.fishergallery.com

Funky Scottish, 41 High Street, Pittenweem, KY10 2PG.
Tel: 01333 312567,
www.funkyscottish.co.uk

Traquairs Gallery, 5 Market Place, Pittenweem, KY10 2PH.
Tel: 01333 311498

LOCAL BUSINESSES

ANSTRUTHER

Accommodation

Waterfront Hotel / Restaurant, 18-20 Shore Street, Anstruther, KY10 3EA. Tel: 01333 312200
www.anstruther-waterfront.co.uk

The Spindrift B&B, Pittenweem Road, Anstruther, KY10 3DT. Tel: 01333 310573, www.thespindrift.co.uk

The Bank Hotel and Restaurant, 23-25 High Street, Anstruther, KY10 3BQ. Tel: 01333 310189, www.thebank-anstruther.co.uk

Crichton House B &B, High Street West, Anstruther, KY10 3DJ. Tel: 01333 310219, www.crichtonhouse.co.uk

Food and Beverage

The Rockies Restaurant, Anstruther Golf Club, Shore Club, Anstruther. Tel: 01333 310981, www.therockiesrestaurant.co.uk

Lisa's Ice Cream Parlour, 23 Shore Street, Anstruther. Tel: 01333 310546

Wee Chippy & Bakehouse Café, 4 Shore Street, Anstruther, KY10 3EA. Tel: 01333 310108

Mrs P's Deli and Coffee Shop, 35 High Street East, Anstruther. Tel: 01333 311931, www.mrsps.co.uk

The Sweetie Shop Takeaway/Café, 9 Rodger Street, Anstruther, KY10 3DU. Tel: 01333 312914

La Petite Epicerie, 32 Cunzie Street, Anstruther, KY10 3DF. Tel: 01333 312179, www.la-petite-epicerie.co.uk

Break Tide Café, 33 Cunzie Street, Anstruther, KY10 3DF. Tel: 01333 312687

Salutation Bar and Lounge, 28 Shore Street, Anstruther. Tel: 01333 312105

Caspian Takeaway, 34 Shore Road, Anstruther, KY10 3AQ. Tel: 01333 312789

The Ship Tavern, 49 Shore Street, Anstruther, KY10 3AQ. Tel: 01333 310347

Salad Bar Takeaway, 38a High Street, Anstruther, KY10 3DH

Anstruther Fish Bar & Restaurant, 44 Shore Street, Anstruther, KY10 3AQ. Tel: 01333 310518, www.ansterfishbar.co.uk

The Dreel Tavern, High Street West, Anstruther, KY10 3DL. Tel: 01333 310727

The Ship Tavern, 49 Shore Street, Anstruther, KY10 3AQ. Tel: 01333 310347

Smugglers Inn, High Street East, Anstruther, KY10 3DQ. Tel: 01333 310506

Post Office

36 Shore Street, Anstruther, KY10 3AQ. Tel: 01333 311984

Medical

Brown T&K Pharmacy, 31-32 Shore Road, Anstruther, KY10 3AQ. Tel: 01333 310322

Banking

ATM, Shore Road, Anstruther, KY10 3AQ

Tourist Attraction

Anstruther Pleasure Cruises, 3 Chalmers Brae, Anstruther, KY10 3BY. Tel: 01333 311808, www.anstrutherpleasurecruises.co.uk

Scottish Fisheries Museum, St. Ayles, Harbourhead, Anstruther, KY10 3AB. Tel: 01333 310628, www.scottishfishmusuem.org

East Neuk Books, 5-7 Rodger Street, Anstruther, KY10 3DU. Tel: 01333 310474

Dos Mundos Fair Trade Clothes, 33 Shore Street, Anstruther, KY10 3AQ. Tel: 01333 313420, www.dosmundos.co.uk

Gibbles Gift Shop, 37 Shore Street, Anstruther, KY10 3AQ, Tel: 01333 313075

Useful Information:

www.anstruther.org.uk

Anstruther to Crail

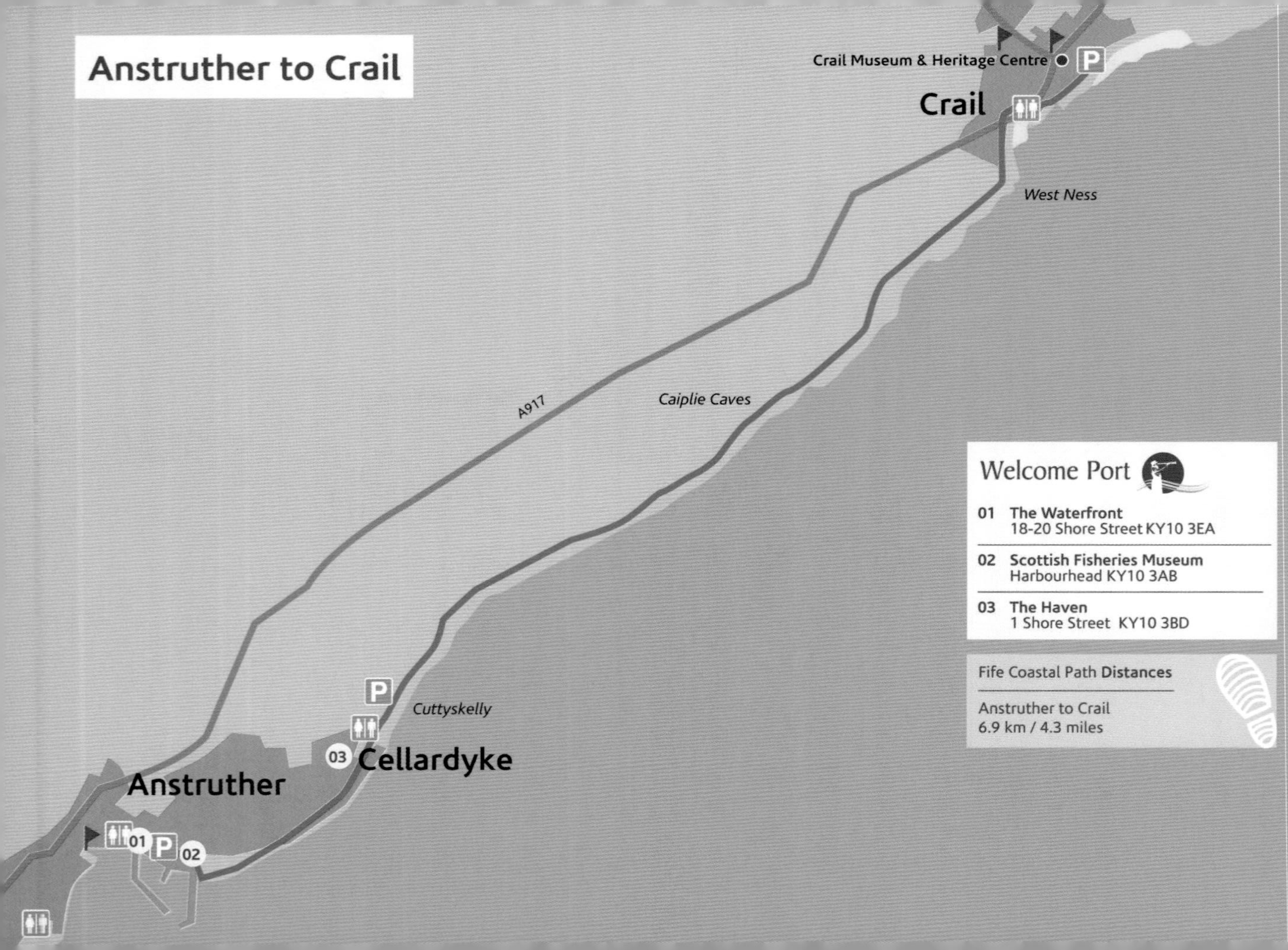

Welcome Port

01 **The Waterfront**
18-20 Shore Street KY10 3EA

02 **Scottish Fisheries Museum**
Harbourhead KY10 3AB

03 **The Haven**
1 Shore Street KY10 3BD

Fife Coastal Path Distances

Anstruther to Crail
6.9 km / 4.3 miles

Crail Museum & Heritage Centre

Crail

West Ness

Caiplie Caves

A917

Cuttyskelly

Cellardyke

03

Anstruther

01 02

CHAPTER FOURTEEN

ANSTRUTHER TO CRAIL

THIS section, which is approximately 4 miles (6.4 km) starts at Anstruther Harbour Car Park and follows the rough, but grassy shoreline to Crail Harbour. It is uneven in parts with rocky stepping-stones in places. Stout footwear should be worn. There are two stone stiles that need to be negotiated and livestock may be present. Dog owners please take care.

Anstruther is actually made up of three Royal Burghs, Anstruther Wester, Anstruther Easter and Cellardyke. It was originally called Kinstrother, meaning 'End of the Marsh'. Each of these burghs has, or had, its own harbour. The Coastal Path signs lead you through the town and past the largest of these, Anstruther Easter.

In the summer months regular boat trips leave from here to the Isle of May. Information on this and other places of interest are available at the nearby Tourist Information Centre that is located next to the Scottish Fisheries Museum, which opened in 1969 and is well worth a visit.

Be sure to have a look and see if the famous herring drifter *The Reaper* is in port when you are in the area. You may also wish to plan your walk so that your route through Anstruther coincides with a mealtime. A fish supper, enjoyed in the open air by the harbour, is a simple treat.

The route continues through the fascinating narrow streets of Cellardyke with stunning views to the Isle of May. A former Royal Burgh of Scotland, from the 11th century to the Reformation, it was the home to the Summer Palace of the Archbishop of St Andrews.

Take the time to visit the picturesque little harbour dating back to the 1400s which was built with the assistance of Dutch builders. The pretty harbour was once home to a large fishing fleet, but is now used mostly for pleasure craft.

At first, the route follows a track that passes a caravan park and an outdoor pig farm. Now a pig farm may not sound all that interesting, but if there are young piglets present they can be very entertaining to watch. These seem to particularly enjoy a game of 'dare' where a group of them will cautiously approach from far behind the fence to look at you before one loses its nerve and the whole group races back to find their mother – squealing loudly with tails held high.

Further on, the path becomes narrower and leads through kissing gates and stone stiles onto open pasture. Livestock may be present in these areas, so please keep dogs under control.

One of the most interesting features along this stretch is the Caiplie Caves. This fascinating geological feature is situated almost halfway between Cellardyke

An interesting stop-off place is the Scottish Fisheries Museum in Anstruther

and Crail, providing an attractive focal point for a short rest.

The caves, located on a raised beach, were once part of a sea cliff. Over time they have been eroded by weather and sea to form the strange, but fascinating shapes we see now. The main cave is called Chapel Cave and it contains some early Christian crosses that have been carved in the sandstone walls. However, care must be taken among the caves now as one of the smaller caves collapsed without warning several years ago.

In spring, wild primroses add a splash of colour to this boulder-strewn coast and these are followed by a progression of wild flowers through the summer months. Scattered shrubs provide cover for nesting birds that include summer visitors such as whitethroat and sedge warbler.

In winter look out for large gatherings of sparrows, finches or starlings, particularly around the pig farm fields.

The route continues past an old saltpan building before winding its way via some stone steps to the scenic village of Crail. As you approach Crail, be sure to have your camera ready for an excellent view of the attractive harbour area, not to be missed by any budding photographer.

Crail became a Royal Burgh in the early 14th century and is a picturesque traditional fishing village whose harbour dates back to at least 1655. The village, like many along the Fife Coast thrived due to its trading links with the Low Countries as far back as the 9th century. Local facilities include public toilets, shops and a small museum, which is well worth a visit.

Caiplie Caves were once part of a sea cliff and can be found between Cellardyke and Crail

Did You Know?
Crail Air Force base

Although Fife has a long and well-known historical relationship with the British military both through the naval dockyard at Rosyth and the Royal Air Force base at Leuchars, what is less well-known is that at one time the East Neuk town of Crail also undertook a similar role. Over the course of the 20th century Crail Aerodrome, standing at the north end of the town, fulfilled varied roles as a naval air station, a flight training school and a language school. To many who passed through the airfield, it was much better known as HMS Jackdaw – a moniker from its World War II days.

It is now recognised as being one of the best surviving examples of World War II airfields of its type – and of a Fleet Air Arm airfield in particular – and as such, the buildings that still stand on the site are now protected by their Scheduled Status under the auspices of Historic Scotland. Although the site of what was once a busy and important airfield is now used for car racing, many of the original buildings can still be seen.

The base at Crail first came to life during the First World War when it was used for training for the Royal Flying Corps. Described by some as the 'eyes' of the Army, the Royal Flying Corps were formed shortly before World War I in 1912 and were used initially for intelligence gathering, such as providing vital reconnaissance through aerial photography and also in the coordination of artillery. As the First World War progressed the squadrons of the Royal Flying Corps were increasingly called into action both in direct fighting against enemy aircraft and in the bombing of strategic German sites.

By the end of the war, the role of aircraft in war times had changed beyond all recognition and the RFC and the Royal Naval Air Service were merged to form the modern day Royal Air Force. Crail Aerodrome played a role in this transformation – in training Royal Flying Corps personnel from 1918–1919 for a role beyond that never imagined prior to 1914.

However, the significance of Crail's Air Force base grew significantly with the advent of World War II. Known as HMS Jackdaw, the Crail Fleet Air Arm airfield was constructed in 1939 and it is the remains of these buildings that can still be viewed today. The Fleet Air Arm is the name given to the division of the Royal Navy responsible for all aspects of naval aircraft. It was formed in 1924 and throughout World War II the Fleet Air Arm also had the responsibility for the protection of the Royal Navy's interests on the ground, one such example being the Naval Base at Rosyth.

The fleet air arm base at Crail played a significant and vital role throughout the war as a torpedo training school, training pilots flying planes with names such as sharks, swordfish, and albacore.

The Fairey Swordfish nicknamed the 'String Bag' – owing to its wire bracings – was a biplane bomber that had great success against U-boats. Much of the intensive training in this skill and that of dive-bombing was undertaken at Crail.

The scale of this training was immense. Official photographs from the time show everything from training in map reading, the fitting of torpedoes, as well as fleets of almost 40 Barracuda aircraft flying over the Forth on their return to Crail after a training mission. The base was also home to `Wrens', who worked on the base packing parachutes and as aircraft mechanics.

In spite of the serious nature of their work, many of those based in Fife throughout the war years have happy memories of the time, speaking of the great sense of camaraderie they felt and the kindness shown to them in Fife.

HMS Jackdaw closed shortly after the end of World War II, but continued to play a military role during the 1950s when it was used as a language school by the Joint Services, training conscripts in languages crucial to the Cold War times, such as Czech, Polish and Russian. The site closed during the 1960s, but the buildings remain, providing a lasting testimony to the role played by Crail Air Force base during the war years.

LOCAL BUSINESSES

CELLARDYKE

Food and Beverage

The Haven Bar, Restaurant and Tea Room, Cellardyke, 01333 310574. www.haven-restaurant.co.uk (Welcome Port)

CRAIL

Accommodation

The Honeypot Guest House and Coffee Shop, 6 High Street South, Crail, KY10 3TD. Tel: 01333 450935. www.thehoneypotcrail.co.uk

Crail Holiday Cottages, Shoregate, Crail, KY10 3SU. Tel: 01333 451896, www.crailholidaycottages.co.uk

Caiplie House B&B, 51-53 High Street North, Crail, KY10 3RA. Tel: 01333 450564, www.caipliehouse.com

Sandcastle Cottage, 3 Nethergate North, Crail, KY10 3TU. Tel: 0131 476401, www.sandcastle-cottage.co.uk

Joyce and Tom Watson B&B, 8 Melville Terrace, Crail, KY10 3EW. Tel: 01333 310453,

The Balcomie Links Hotel, Balcomie Road, Crail, KY10 3TN. Tel: 01333 450237, www.balcomie.co.uk

The East Neuk Hotel, 67 High Street North, Crail, KY10 3RA. Tel: 01333 450225

The Hazelton Guest House, 29 Marketgate North, Crail. Tel: 01333 450250, www.thehazelton.co.uk

The Golf Hotel, 4 High Street, Crail, KY10 3TD. Tel: 01333 450206, www.thegolfhotelcrail.com

Selcraig House, 47 Nethergate, Crail, KY10 3TX. Tel: 01333 450697, www.selcraighouse.co.uk

Food and Beverage

Barnet's the Baker, 24 High Street, Crail, Fife, KY10 3ET. Tel: 01333 451953

Julia's Eatery and Gifts, 36 High Street, Crail, KY10 3RB. Tel: 01333 450415

Beehive Confectioner and Souvenirs, 28 High Street South, Crail, KY10 3TE. Tel: 01333 450330

Co-op, 7 High Street North, Crail, Fife, KY10 3TA. Tel: 01333 450309

K&B Foodstore, 2 High Street South, Crail. Tel: 01333 451818

First Fruits, 14 High Street, Crail, KY10 3TD. Tel: 01333 450010

The Lobster Store, 34 Shoregate, Crail, KY10 3SU. Tel: 01333 450476

Banking

ATM, 31 Marketgate North, Crail, KY10 3UG

Medical

Crail Pharmacy, 18 High Street South, Crail, KY10 3TE. Tel: 01333 450402

Post Office

Crail Post Office, 41 High Street North, Crail, K10 3RA. Tel: 01333 450200

Tourist Attraction

Crail Museum, 62-64 Marketgate South, Crail, KY10 3TL. Tel: 01333 450869, www.crailmuseum.org.uk

Galleries and Gift Shops

Crail Book Shop, 61 High Street, Crail, KY10 3RA.

Crail Gallery, 22 High Street, Fife, KY10 3RA. Tel: 01333 450 316, www.crailgallery.com

Crail Harbour Gallery and Tearoom, Shoregate, Crail, KY10 3SU. Tel: 01333 451896, www.crailharbourgallery.co.uk

The Jerden Gallery, 42 Marketgate South, Crail. Tel: 01333 450797, www.thejerdengallery.com

Useful information

www.aboutcrail.co.uk

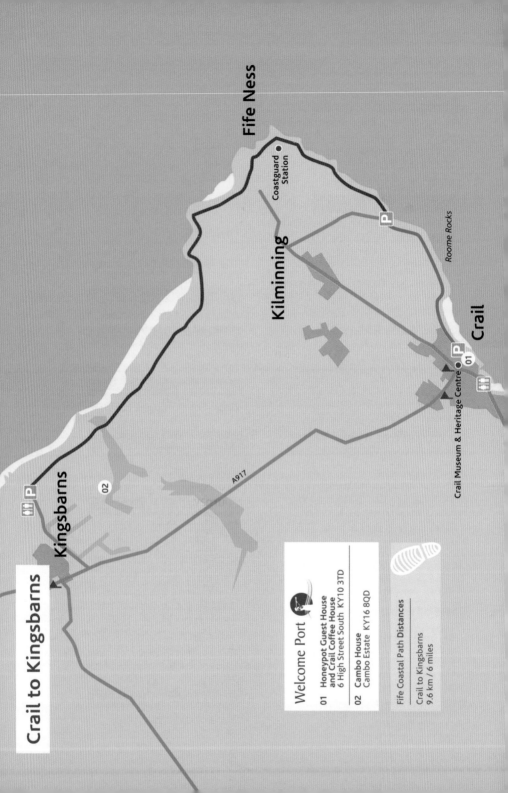

Crail to Kingsbarns

Fife Ness

Kilminning

Coastguard
Station

Roome Rocks

Crail

Crail Museum & Heritage Centre

Kingsbarns

A917

Welcome Port

01 Honeypot Guest House
    and Crail Coffee House
    6 High Street South KY10 3TD

02 Cambo House
    Cambo Estate KY16 8QD

Fife Coastal Path Distances

Crail to Kingsbarns
9.6 km / 6 miles

CHAPTER FIFTEEN

CRAIL TO KINGSBARNS

THIS section, which starts at Crail Harbour, is approximately 6 miles (9.6 km) in length and ends at the Coastal Path Car Park, Kingsbarns Beach. It crosses a wide variety of path conditions, from tarmac road to very rough rocky shore. Needless to say, good sturdy footwear is essential. There is one tidal point, so check tide times before setting out. Livestock may be present on parts of this stretch so, dog owners please keep your pets under close control.

The route begins by leading you round Roome Bay at the north-eastern edge of the village. This is an attractive beach, which is very popular with visitors in the summer.

After Roome Bay the route continues through Sauchope Caravan Park before emerging onto a narrower and altogether rougher section of path.

Soon it enters Kilminning Wildlife Reserve. The Scottish Wildlife Trust maintains this and part of the site's management involves grazing sheep or cattle at certain times of year. If you have a dog, please keep it on a lead and under close control.

The shore now becomes rougher, with a prominent sandstone outcrop near the start of the reserve, called Kilminning Castle. Follow the route through the reserve and onto Fife Ness, which is the most easterly point in Fife. This is an excellent area for bird watching particularly during spring and autumn. This is when numbers of migratory birds regularly turn up together with an occasional rarity. The blackthorn and bramble scrub provides welcome shelter where exhausted birds can rest and feed before continuing on their journey.

There is a coastguard station and associated buildings here and the path continues beneath them. To the right, it passes an old WWII gun emplacement and a Fife Bird Club hide (members only so this is usually locked). The path then joins a narrow tarmac road that passes some caravans.

There was once a small harbour here. Nearby there was a small tidal mill and a circular rock template that once was used as a guide for building lighthouse towers. Information panels tell you more.

You'll pass through Kilminning Wildlife Reserve as you walk the Fife Coastal Path

After a short distance the road turns inland and the route leaves it to follow the coast, once more becoming a sandy, narrow path. It now runs along the boundary of the Crail Golfing Society golf course, one of the oldest courses in the world. Follow safety signs and keep alert to what golfers around you are doing.

The path passes Constantine's Cave, a site with early Christian wall carvings as well as where archaeological investigations unearthed Roman Pottery. Nearby you will also see more WWII outposts, including a curious metal egg-shaped container now half-buried in the sand.

Beyond the golf course the route again becomes rougher as it crosses a stile and continues along the shore beneath the cliffs of Randerston. This is the tidal part of the route so the timing of the walk should have been carefully planned to avoid difficulty or delay. Fulmars nest here in summer and their calls can sound eerily atmospheric as they echo down from the rocky ledges above.

These birds, which also nest on rocky cliffs around Crail and St Andrews, have an interesting and effective defence against predators or intruders who get too close. Both adults and young can eject a foul smelling substance over unwelcome visitors.

Fulmars are also interesting because although they are similar in colour and size to a gull they are actually more closely related to the albatross.

This fact reminds me of an amusing exchange which happened when I was showing some schoolchildren a pair of fulmars at their nest. I asked the children what they thought the birds were, to which all replied: 'Seagulls'. 'No', I said. `They may look like gulls, but do any of you know what an albatross is?' Quick as a flash one little boy put his hand up and said, 'Yes, I know – it's three under par!' No surprise then to learn that this particular group of children had come from the home of golf – St Andrews.

The grassy area beyond the cliffs is used for grazing cattle in summer, so again it is important to keep your dog under control. It is probably better in any case to keep to the beach until a stone wall is reached which marks the boundary between Randerston and the relatively new Kingsbarns Golf Links.

A built-in stone stile helps you cross the wall and once over you have a choice of route. The low tide route keeps to the shore whilst the high tide follows a rise inland. Though slightly longer, the latter offers particularly attractive views and is a rewarding diversion whatever the state of the tide.

The routes join up near the foot of Cambo Den where there are further diversions along an alternative route, as well as woodland walks, which are provided by the estate. Cambo is famous for its wonderful display of snowdrops in early spring so, at that time of year, a wander into the Den can be difficult to resist.

The main coastal route continues along a sandy golf maintenance track that runs through the dunes, but if the tide is out, the golden sands of Kingsbarns Beach

Plenty of wildlife interest at Kingsbarns Beach - especially at low tide

may prove to be the bigger attraction. Here too, there is real wildlife interest. The rock pools abound with all sorts of intertidal life, while shore birds such as redshank, turnstone and oystercatcher favour the boulder strewn shallows around the south-east end of the bay.

Whether you are following the beach, the dunes or the alternative route you will soon arrive at Kingsbarns Car Park where there is an information panel, picnic tables and litterbins.

Refreshments and bus stops are available in Kingsbarns village that can be reached by following the road that joins the car park for approximately one kilometre.

LOCAL BUSINESSES

KINGSBARNS

Accommodation

Kingsbarns B&B, 3 Main Street, Kingsbarns, KY16 8SL. Tel: 01334 880234, www.kingsbarnsb-b.co.uk

Cambo House, Cambo Estate, Kingsbarns, KY16 8QD. Tel: 01333 450054, www.camboestate.com

Pitmilly West Lodge B&B, Kingsbarns, KY16 8AQ. Tel: 01334 88058, www.staykingsbarns.com

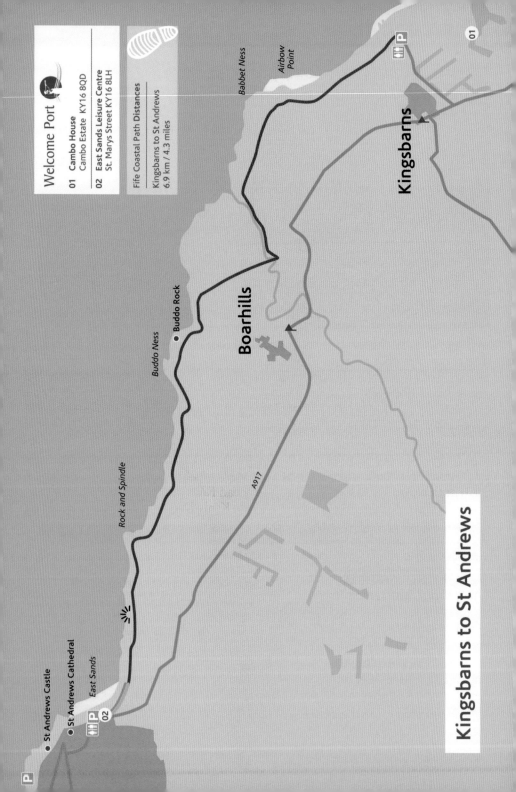

Welcome Port

01 Cambo House
Cambo Estate KY16 8QD

02 East Sands Leisure Centre
St. Marys Street KY16 8LH

Fife Coastal Path Distances

Kingsbarns to St Andrews
6.9 km / 4.3 miles

Babbet Ness

Airbow
Point

Kingsbarns

Buddo Ness

• Buddo Rock

Boarhills

Rock and Spindle

A917

• St Andrews Castle

• St Andrews Cathedral

East Sands

02

P

Kingsbarns to St Andrews

CHAPTER SIXTEEN

KINGSBARNS TO ST ANDREWS

THIS section is roughly 7.5 miles (12 km) in length and starts at Kingsbarns Car Park. It follows a beautiful, lonely stretch of coast, which is rough in places and parts of it can become very muddy, particularly in winter, so stout footwear should be worn. It may also feel much longer due to the many ups and downs and the rough terrain.

It is tidal in places so check tides before setting off. Dog owners should take care, as livestock may be present.

The section begins by following a track along Kingsbarns Golf Links, (again, follow advice on safety notices). Soon a stone wall is reached where steps cross over to a much narrower path beyond. Now the golf course is left behind and the route hugs the coastal slope between rocky shore and farmland.

The narrow path soon descends down to join the shore that now becomes sandy and provides relatively easy walking. Follow the beach, past a green cabin and on to Babbet Ness where the route once more becomes a narrow sandy path.

This part of the coast sometimes has a remote, slightly bleak feel, but it is also excellent for wildlife and there is almost always something to see. Wading birds are common along the shore, eider and sometimes shelduck can be seen a little further out while in summer wildflowers such as knapweed, campions and vetches provide a splash of colour alongside the path.

Eventually the route widens and becomes a grassy track, which turns inland at the mouth of the Kenly Burn, towards Hillhead Farm. It then veers right, down some stone steps, to join the path through the Kenly Den.

This wooded den offers a real contrast to the open, windswept landscape of the Kingsbarns coast. In early spring there are carpets of snowdrops that are later replaced by bluebells and primroses, whilst you can often spot birds such as dippers or grey wagtails along the riverbank.

The route passes an old mill and continues upstream until it crosses a bridge near Burnside Farm. It then follows farm tracks through arable farmland until reaching the outskirts of Boarhills. Here the path skirts the edge of the village, passing Boarhills Farm before heading back down to the coast.

If you wish to explore the village, bear in mind that there is no shop, café or pub in Boarhills to offer refreshments. However there is a bus stop with regular services to St Andrews.

It often seems to be the case in Scotland that the most beautiful landscapes are also the most challenging. This certainly applies to Boarhills to St Andrews,

Buddo Rock, above, is an impressive stack of pink sandstone and left, Kenly Den

which may be the roughest section of the whole route but is also undeniably one of the most attractive.

The route is tidal so tide times should be checked beforehand and stout footwear should be worn. Some parts are prone to become extremely muddy during wet winter weather so, in these conditions, waterproof trousers or gaiters may also be useful.

Follow the track from Boarhills Farm down through fields to the coast. After crossing a timber stile a grassy slope leads to the path that follows the rugged shoreline west towards St Andrews.

The first point of interest is Buddo Rock, an impressive stack of pink sandstone, which once formed part of the cliffs of a raised beach.

The path continues, rising up the bank and following a stone wall before falling to the shore again. The going again becomes rougher just before Kittocks Den. Here the path is narrow and can become slippery in wet conditions, so care should be taken.

The path meets the shore at the foot of Kittocks Den and here it is worth pausing to look at the vegetation. The wet conditions enable a variety of mosses, ferns and liverworts to thrive.

The path soon climbs once more to eventually run alongside the golf course at St Andrews Bay. Here the view of the clubhouse and hotel surrounded by well-kept grounds, greens and fairways contrast greatly with the wildness of the adjacent coast. The views from here are superb on a clear day and if the sea is really calm it can be worth looking out for seals, porpoises or even bottlenose dolphins.

Soon the path starts to drop again, through a natural tunnel formed by

The Rock and Spindle is a point of interest on the shoreline overlooking St Andrews Bay

blackthorn shrubs, until it once more reaches the shore. The next point of interest can soon be seen ahead, the Rock and Spindle.

This is a striking geological feature. The 'spindle' consists of radiating basalt rays while the 'rock' is a weathered volcanic plug, formed millions of years ago. The path follows the shore before continuing along an undulating stone path that passes the Rock and Spindle and follows the shore to the next bay. Livestock often graze this area, so keep dogs on leads.

The grazing clears away the rougher grasses, so that the more delicate plants have a better chance to thrive. The results can be seen in early summer when the area is brightened by the splash of colour provided by primroses, bluebells and orchids. Soon the path crosses a stile and climbs a flight of stone steps to the area known as Kinkell Braes. The view of St Andrews is much closer now and before long, Kinkell Caravan Park is in sight. The grassy slopes here are a haven for rabbits and the shrubs form a popular roosting site for linnets and other finches.

Near the caravan park the path passes an altogether more recent geological feature. This is a landslip, which has been active over recent years and has resulted in the path having to be moved ever further inland. Between the path and the slip there is a large area of self-seeded buddleia. On sunny summer days this is an excellent place to observe a wonderful variety of butterflies and bumblebees as they feed from the nectar rich blossoms.

The path now follows the edge of the caravan park before dropping down to join the tarmac path that continues through the historic town of St Andrews.

This marks the end of my section of the Fife Coastal Path. I hope you have enjoyed it as much as I always do. The Coastal Path is a wonderful asset not just to Fife but to Scotland as well. Intensely varied, there is always something new to discover no matter how many times you've walked the route. I'll pass you on now to my colleague, Ranald who will lead you on the next part of your journey along the Fife Coastal Path.

Did You Know?
The Scottish Outdoor Access Code

In a country as beautiful and diverse as Scotland, it seems fitting that we also have one of the most liberal approaches in the world to outdoor access – ensuring that the landscape is there to be enjoyed by everyone.

From Fife's spectacular coastline to the rugged mountains of the Highlands and from the forests of Perthshire to the sea cliffs of Shetland, visitors can explore in the knowledge that they have a statutory right of responsible access, defined by the Scottish Outdoor Access Code.

The Scottish Outdoor Access Code came into being in February 2005, as a direct result of the Land Reform (Scotland) Act of 2003. This marked the end of years of work by many public bodies, local authorities, campaigning groups and individuals, to get clarity and consistency on rights of access in Scotland.

This was viewed as being particularly important, as Scotland had always enjoyed a reputation as a country where people enjoyed good 'rights to roam'. Increasing pressures, including greater public awareness of 'the great outdoors' shed light on a complicated, often localised, approach, which left outdoor enthusiasts baffled as to what they could and couldn't do and land owners and managers often feeling that they lacked information and support too. And, with New Labour entering Westminster in 1997 with health, sustainability and the environment high on their agenda, it was clear that something had to be done.

The work of the National Access Forum – established in 1994 – had already brought together a number of key players and highlighted fundamental issues, setting the scene for Scottish Natural Heritage (SNH) to take up the mantle of drafting the first ever Scottish outdoor access legislation.

Following the Code's wise advice to 'Know the Code before You Go', the broad principles are set out below.

Everyone has the statutory right of access.

Access rights apply to all land and inland waters, unless excluded.

Access rights are for outdoor recreation, for crossing land and water and for some educational and commercial purposes.

Exercising access rights and managing access land, must be done responsibly.

Where access rights do not apply.

Houses and gardens and non-residential buildings with their associated land.

Farm buildings and yards.

Land in which crops have been sown or are growing (although please note the headrigs, endrigs and other margins of fields where crops are growing are not defined as crops, whether sown or unsown and are therefore within access rights).

Land next to a school and used by the school.

Sports or playing fields when these are in use and where the exercise of access rights would interfere with such use.

Land developed and in use for recreation and where the exercise of access rights would interfere with such use.

Golf courses (but you can cross a golf course provided you don't interfere with any games of golf).

Places like airfields, railways, telecommunication sites, military bases and installations, working quarries and construction sites.

Visitor attractions or other places that charge for entry.

For comprehensive information on the Code visit http://www.outdooraccess-scotland.com

LOCAL BUSINESSES

BOARHILLS

Accommodation

Mill Cottage Self Catering,
Mill House, Boarhills, KY16 8PS.
Tel: 01334 880254,
www.parkmill-cottages.co.uk

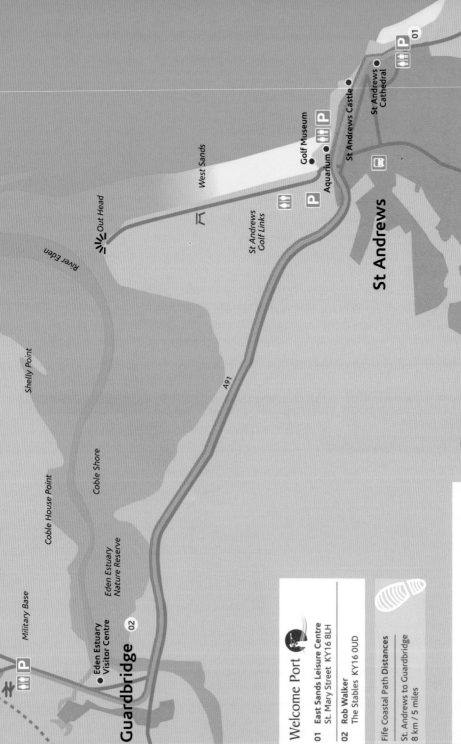

River Eden

Out Head

West Sands

Shelly Point

Coble House Point

Coble Shore

Eden Estuary Nature Reserve

Military Base

Eden Estuary Visitor Centre

Guardbridge 02

A91

St Andrews Golf Links

Golf Museum

Aquarium

St Andrews Castle

St Andrews Cathedral

St Andrews

01

Welcome Port

01 East Sands Leisure Centre
St. Mary Street KY16 8LH

02 Rob Walker
The Stables KY16 0UD

Fife Coastal Path Distances

St. Andrews to Guardbridge
8 km / 5 miles

St Andrews to Guardbridge

CHAPTER SEVENTEEN

ST ANDREWS TO GUARDBRIDGE

MY name is Ranald Strachan and I have been a Ranger for several years. Growing up in a concrete jungle housing estate in Edinburgh gave me a great desire to seek out green and natural places. At first this was through sports such as mountaineering, cycling and kayaking. Through this interface with wild and natural places, I cultivated a strong and lasting interest in the countryside of Scotland. Why is it what it is? What makes it so and how it is subject to our influence?

Countryside Ranger
Ranald Strachan

This led to working as an arborist for many years, which in turn grew into a passion for more than just trees. I wanted to be 'involved' with the countryside and learn more about how it works and even try and enhance it for the benefit of its intrinsic value as our national asset and also to promote this asset to others to assist in its future conservation. This led to me becoming a Countryside Ranger. I believe the work Countryside Rangers do acts as a bridge between the social, cultural and natural parts of our heritage.

My favourite stretch is between Tayport and Newport. It is easily accessible, gentle and has a passive charm that allows a bit of restful reflection. Walking along Scotland's greatest river, the Tay, following an old branch line that once carried steam trains to the ferry ports and the doomed crossing of McGonagall's 'Railway Bridge of the Silvery Tay'.

The walk takes you past quaint, old, redundant lighthouses and railway relics with the Tay at your feet and views stretching up into the estuary and out to the North Sea. Bottlenose dolphins are a regular sight close in by the wee harbour and there is plenty of birdlife to see. A nice coffee can be had at either end too!

This section of the Fife Coastal Path stretches for 5 miles (7.5 km). Beginning in the ancient and historic town of St Andrews at the East Sands Leisure Centre Car Park it leads to Guardbridge, a village situated on the crossing point of the River Eden. The coastline softens considerably from St Andrews and your path travels through an area of low-lying country rich in history and heritage both cultural and natural. The walking is easy and the views are panoramic.

For the next five miles you will be on tarmac, making for simple walking, reasonable for bikes and pushchairs although there are some steep hills to negotiate. This section starts at the first of the 'Sands' of St Andrews.

East Sands is a fine beach popular with surfers, sailors and kayakers. Open to the North Sea and with a steep profile the beach produces some fantastic waves when the tide is in; when the tide is out it's great for 'guddling' around in the rock pools.

Leaving the East Sands, cross the swinging harbour bridge and head around the harbour, still a thriving fishery landing lobster and Dublin Bay prawn.

If, like me, you have a salty sea dog yearning, here's a good spot to indulge in a bit of seaside atmosphere. Grab an ice cream, watch the boats and drift away to the sounds of the gulls and waves.

At the northern end of the harbour take the winding route up towards the imposing ruins of the medieval cathedral. Standing alongside the cathedral and

East Sands is a popular beach with surfers

most impressive, is St Rules Tower.

The cliff top setting of the path at this point is spectacular. Below, there is plenty to see, eider duck in amongst the skerries and the stiff-winged fulmar nesting along the cliffs. The eye is drawn to the medieval ruins and it is highly recommended to take some time to enjoy the scene and absorb a bit of the rich history that include Pictish burials, religious relics, kings and some notable murders.

A short distance on brings you to the Scores and the ruins of St Andrews Castle. Sitting above the Castle Sands and managed by Historic Scotland, a fee is

The imposing ruins of the mediaeval St Andrews Cathedral

required to enter the castle. Built around 1200 the weathered fortification seems to melt into the worn orange sandstone cliffs below.

The castle is worth a visit as contained inside is the famous 'Bottle Dungeon' and even more spectacular is the mine shaft built during the siege of 1546, incidentally only six years before the first reference to golf was made in the town.

Travelling along The Scores to Golf Place you leave behind the crags and cliffs of the East Neuk and drop into the wide low-lying lands of the north-east corner of Fife.

Laid out before you is The Old Course and stretching away to the horizon is the expanse of West Sands – the largest and most dramatic of the Sands of St Andrews. A spectacular beach, famous as the venue for the filming of Chariots of Fire and in more recent times the site of some innovative sand dune restoration works.

The Old Course clubhouse, home to the Royal and Ancient Golf Club and the Golf Museum both lie on Golf Place and if the ancient game is one of your interests a stop here is recommended. There is a good toilet by the museum too! Alternatively, why not spend a while exploring the town itself?

St Andrews is home to the famous university, founded in 1412, which was the first in Scotland. St Andrews also offers some lovely places to stop and rest while enjoying one of the many restaurants or coffee shops. Once you have explored the town, head back towards Hamilton Hall and the 18th Green to continue your journey.

Crossing Golf Place head down the western side of the Old Course towards the Old Course Hotel. Visible here is the famous Swilken Bridge and if no golf is being played, pop over and admire this wee bit of Fife history and get a photo of you on the bridge, just like Jack Nicklaus, Tony Jacklin or Tiger Woods. The Old Course is closed to golf on Sundays, a good day to visit.

The next mile is dominated by the St Andrews golf courses, giving great views across the Links, home to a sizeable population of brown hare. By the road entrance to the Pilmuir at the end of the north playing fields, the path joins the cycleway to Guardbridge.

This is a flat and pleasant walk through farmland with wide-open views of the Eden Estuary. On leaving St Andrews you can reflect on how much of a coastal town it is. This can be demonstrated in full when the town is enveloped in haar sea mist and when a strong easterly blows, you can hear the roar and smell the salt spray in the town centre.

To the south across the main A91 the land rises in a single step. This is a raised beach left high and dry by the raising of the land and dropping of the sea level after the last Ice Age. The fields to the north of the path are great places in winter to spot large flocks of waders such as golden plover or lapwing.

A pair of binoculars would provide the walker with the opportunity to enjoy the estuary that lies quietly to the north. The path now descends slowly into Guardbridge before crossing the River Eden by way of the ancient Gaire Brig of the mid 15th century. This bridge carries the Arms of James Beaton, one time Archbishop of St Andrews and weighty historical dude. Designed to replace an even older ford that ran below its six attractive arches the medieval bridge carried traffic right up to 1939, when the more modern bridge finally gave it some peace.

To the west, the stumps of the old railway bridge remain. The bridge is now only for foot and cycle use and is a lovely vantage point to view the wildlife of the River Eden. This is a regular spot for otter and is a fine place to watch dabbling ducks and let your mind drift off downstream. Take a minute here.

West Sands, at St Andrews was where the Chariots of Fire movie was filmed

Did You Know?
History of golf in Fife

For many visitors to Fife – particularly those from international destinations – the lure is that of 18, possibly 19, holes on some of the best and most renowned golf courses in the world. With images of The Old Course at St Andrews filtering on to television screens in homes all over the planet, it's not surprising that the moniker 'The Home of Golf' is most associated with this corner of Scotland.

Golf in St Andrews can be traced back as far as the mid-1500s and the Royal and Ancient states that by 1691 St Andrews was already known as the 'metropolis of golfing'. And having hosted The Open more times than any other golf course, since it hosted its first in 1873, the Old Course has won a place in the hearts of all who have played there, with golfing greats such as Jack Nicklaus and Tiger Woods marking it among their favourites.

There's much more to golf in Fife than the Old Course itself. The very history and beginnings of the game are rooted in the area. The most early and primitive form of golf involved a game of knocking small stones into rabbit holes and it was particularly popular in coastal areas where the lay of the land – the links area – lent itself to flatter and more open spaces for this sport.

In fact, so popular was this game that in March of 1457, King James II of Scotland banned football and 'ye golf' as it was distracting his young subjects from their archery practice. By 1552 however, the battle was lost and an Act of Parliament pronounced the legal right to play golf on the links land in St Andrews – land that is now the site of the Old Course itself. From here, golf gained strength and popularity to the extent that there are now no less than 11 courses in the St Andrews area and an astounding 50 in the county of Fife.

One of the best-known names in golf is also associated with Fife with the Royal and Ancient Golf Club having its origins in St Andrews.

Dating back to 1754 the club became known as the official governing body of golf, a role that it undertook until 2003, along with the responsibility for organising the British Open. In 2004 these powers were devolved to a new body called the R&A which now upholds the rules of golf – in conjunction with its American counterpart – as well as undertaking a range of activities in pursuit of maintaining the world class reputation of golf.

But if there's one character whose image is synonymous with the town of St Andrews and whose history is intertwined with that of golf in Fife, it's Old Tom Morris.

Born in St Andrews in 1821 Tom Morris began playing golf at an early age and started his career in golf in his teenage years as a caddy for one of the best professionals of the day. His reputation as a superb golfer spread far and wide, but his role as a pioneer of modern professional golf was secured when he designed and maintained a golf course in Prestwick. His career flourished and he became influential in all aspects of the game, from designing clubs and balls to coaching and even organising The Open.

He returned to St Andrews in 1865 where he is credited with transforming the course bringing his wisdom to widen the fairways and manage the grounds to his own exacting standards, many of which form the basis for green-keeping today. Beyond St Andrews, Old Tom Morris' golf course designs can be seen across Scotland, with Fife course, Balcomie, at Crail also bearing his mark.

The legacy of Tom Morris – as a designer, green-keeper and professional – is evident throughout the golfing world and nowhere more clearly than in Fife. The man himself died in St Andrews in 1908 and his grave can still be seen in the grounds of St Andrews Cathedral.

LOCAL BUSINESSES

ST ANDREWS

Accommodation

Fairmont St Andrews, St Andrews, Fife, KY16 8PN. Tel: 01334 837000, www.fairmont.com/standrews

St Andrews Holiday Park, St Andrews, KY9 1HB. Tel: 01333 330283, www.abbeyford.com

Ardgowan Hotel, 2 Playfair's Terrace, St Andrews, KY16 9HX. Tel: 01334 472970, www.ardgowanhotel.co.uk

Annandale Guest House, 23 Murray Park, St Andrews, KY16 9AW. Tel: 01334 475310, www.annandale-standrews.com

Castlemount B&B, 2 The Scores, St Andrews, KY16 9AR. Tel: 01334 475579, www.castlemount.net

Glendarran Guesthouse, 9 Murray Park, St Andrews, KY16 9AW. Tel: 01334 477951, www.glenderran.com

MacDonald Rusacks Hotel, Pilmour Links, St Andrews, KY16 9JQ. Tel: 0844 8799136, www.macdonaldhotels.co.uk/Rusacks

Braeside House B&B, 25 Nelson Street, St Andrews, KY16 8AJ. Tel: 01334 473375, www.braeside-standrews.co.uk

LOCAL BUSINESSES

ST ANDREWS

Accommodation (cont)

St Nicholas Farmhouse B&B, The Steadings, East Sands, St Andrews, KY16 8LD. Tel: 01334 473090, www.stnicholasfarmhouse.com

Old Course Hotel, Golf Resort and Spa, Old Station Road, St Andrews, KY16 9SP. Tel: 01334 474371, www.oldcoursehotel.co.uk

Ivybank Self Catering, 41 Lade Braes, St Andrews, KY16 9DA. Tel: 01344 626431, www.ascotmatters.co.uk/ivybank

The Spindle B&B, 4 Dempster Terrace, St Andrews, KY16 9QQ. Tel: 01334 477185, www.thespindle.co.uk

Five Pilmour Place, 5 Pilmour Place, St Andrews, KY16 9HZ. Tel: 01334 478665, www.5pilmourplace.com

Milton Lea B&B, Milton Lea, St Andrews, KY16 0AB. Tel:05602 988677, www.miltonlea.co.uk

Acorn B&B, 16 Priestden Road, St Andrews. Tel: 01334 476009, www.acorn.standrews.btinternet.co.uk

Best Western Scores, 76 The Scores, St Andrews, KY16 9BB. Tel: 01334 472451, www.bw-scoreshotel.co.uk

NO 12 B&B, 12 Grange Road, St Andrews, KY16 8LF Tel: 01334 471949, www.no12bedandbreakfaststandrews.co.uk

Food and Beverage

Taste Coffee Shop, 148 North Street, St Andrews. Tel: 01334 477959

Fritto Fish and Chips, 1-3 Union Street, St Andrews. KY16 9PQ. Tel: 01334 475555

Northpoint Café, 24 North Street, St Andrews. Tel: 01334 473997

Jannetta Ice Cream and Café, 31 South Street, St Andrews, KY16 9QR. Tel: 01334 473285, www.jannettas.co.uk

Tourist Attraction

St Andrews Preservation Trust Museum, 12 North Street, St Andrews, KY16 9PW 01334 477629, www.standrewspreservationtrust.org

Museum of the University of St Andrews, 7a The Scores, St Andrews, KY16 9AR. Tel: 01334 461660, www.st-andrews.ac.uk/about/museumsand collections/MUSA

St Andrews Aquarium, The Scores, St Andrews, KY16 9AS. Tel: 01334 474786, www.standrewsaquarium.co.uk

British Golf Museum, Bruce Embankment, St Andrews, KY16 9AB Tel: 01334 460046, www.britishgolfmuseum.co.uk

Banking

ATM, South Street, St Andrews, KY16 9QB.

Galleries and Gift Shops

Beetle Belinda, 16 Bell Street, St Andrews, KY16 9UX. Tel: 01334 472286

GUARDBRIDGE

Accommodation

The Larches B&B, 7 River Terrace, Guardbridge, KY16 0XA. Tel: 01334 838008

Food and Beverage

Dalis Takeaway, 2 Cupar Road, Guardbridge, KY16 0UA. Tel: 01334 839797

Antique Furniture

Rob Walker Furniture, The Stables, Guardbridge, KY16 0UD. Tel. 01334 838217

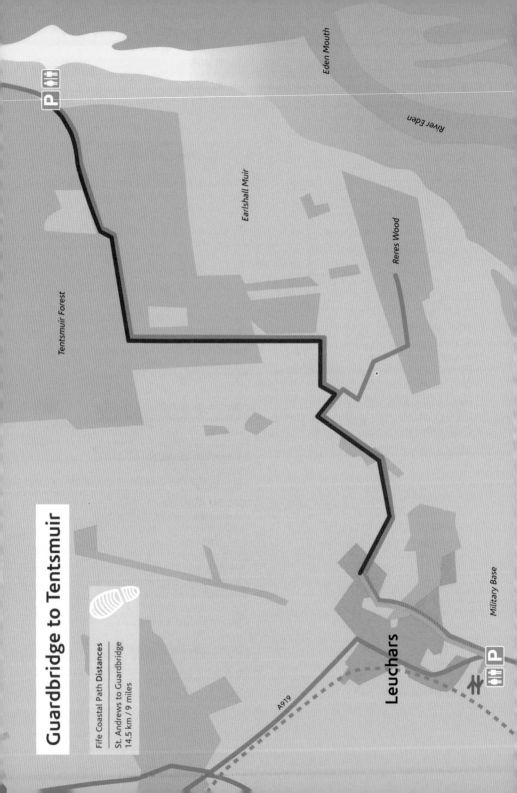

Guardbridge to Tentsmuir

Fife Coastal Path Distances

St. Andrews to Guardbridge
14.5 km / 9 miles

Tentsmuir Forest

Earlshall Muir

Eden Mouth

River Eden

Reres Wood

Leuchars

Military Base

A919

CHAPTER EIGHTEEN

GUARDBRIDGE TO TENTSMUIR

THIS section of the Fife Coastal Path is approximately 9 miles (13.5 km) and begins in the busy crossroads village of Guardbridge by the main crossing of the River Eden. Car parking can be had along Old St Andrews Road and a sizeable layby provides free parking. This section follows roads until you go through Leuchars where the character changes dramatically as you pass the military base of Leuchars, out onto the open and 'wild' feeling Earlshall Muir before entering Tentsmuir Forest. The walking is fairly easy with a small amount of rough track across Earlshall Muir. This is a varied section leading back towards the Tentsmuir coast.

Guardbridge has always been a meeting place and as such trade and industry has been its history. The Pilgrims' 'gaire brig' stands at an important junction where travellers can go south to Cupar, east to St Andrews and north to Dundee. Once a busy port, the village and the Eden Estuary nearby, have had a long relationship. Up until the Victorian Age schooners came up to this 'Water of Eden' port.

Once over the ancient crossing, cross the main A919 to follow the path as it leads quietly behind houses to the site of the former paper mill. A highly recommended detour should be taken along the Main Street (A919) of the village to visit the Eden Estuary Centre. This is great facility secreted at the back of the Main Street Park.

The centre gives fantastic views over the Eden Estuary Nature Reserve and is a great spot to get up close to the birdlife, so abundant on the estuary. This is another good place to rest, cool the feet off and blether to some locals. The visitors here believe this to be the best bird hide in Scotland The best time to visit the Eden Estuary is when the tide is half in, or half out. This can allow for unbelievably close views of some usually enigmatic birds. This is a true spectacle, especially during the winter months. Bring a camera.

Head along the main street of Guardbridge, past the paper mill that was built on the old Seggie distillery site and started operating as a paper mill in 1873. A village was built to house the mill workers on reclaimed land from the Eden and hence Guardbridge was born. Sadly the mill closed in 2008 and a community lost its main employer. However efforts are being made to redevelop the site and in time it is hoped that Guardbridge will once again have a focus to push this busy little community into a new future.

Crossing the reed beds of the Motray Water by way of the Inner Bridge, the walker's attention will be drawn to the proximity of the Leuchars Military Base.

View across the Eden Estuary

Crossing the A919 onto the Leuchars Road and at the crest of a short hill, a view straight across the base will no doubt impress. Look into the skies and recall the days when the RAF flew out of here in the dark days of the 1940s.

This was when boys from Guardbridge used to wave at the pilots taking off over this vantage point and they would sometimes be offered a chance to hop the fence and get a jolly around the skies of Guardbridge. Changed days now!

The path continues passing the main gate of the Leuchars base, which has a long and interesting history and has been involved in many operations over the years. It was used mainly as an RAF base while squadrons flew out of Leuchars to intercept German bombers, Russian spy planes and provide air support for conflicts overseas.

The path then takes a turn up Wessex Avenue and visible in the distance is the beautiful Kirk of St Athernase. A short detour would take you to this church, with its Romanesque features. It was built in 1183-87 and stands in proud relief in the centre of the village and is well worth a visit. It is truly unique.

The path turns off Wessex Avenue and here the mood changes. Earlshall Road has a charm all of its own, a classic country lane that leads past some fine hedgerows and old ash trees to the attractive woodland setting of Earlshall

Castle. This castle is private property however it can be easily viewed and the splendid grounds appreciated from the road. Watch out for the strange and rather grotesque gate adornments.

Continue on through the farm gate by the base fence and through a copse of birch trees favoured in winter by flocks of greenfinches, past the Comerton motor cross track and through a second gate out past a plantation of Scots pine.

The path now opens out into the wild expanse of Earlshall Muir. According to medieval chronicles a place of 'devils, bears and oxen' and 'a place best avoided'. I disagree. The Muir is home to lapwings and curlew now, birds that carry dark folklore in Fife. The lapwing apparently cries 'Bewitched! Bewitched!' and the curlew is the 'night crier' that 'carries off the unwary soul'. Fitting tales for a lonely and wild dune heath.

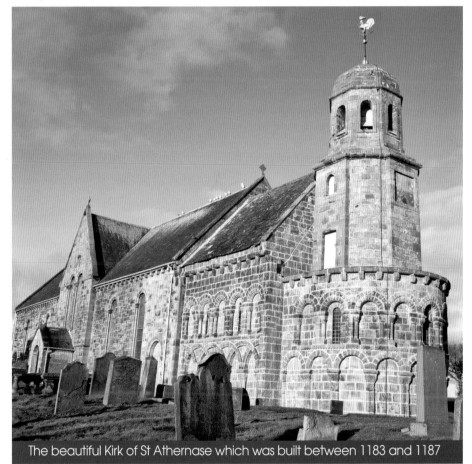

The beautiful Kirk of St Athernase which was built between 1183 and 1187

Please take time to appreciate the desolate feel of this Muir. This kind of landscape is very atmospheric and harks of wild outlaws, shipwrecks and lost travellers. This landscape is becoming very rare indeed and with its slow disappearance that special wild and remote feeling goes with it.

We all need a wee bit more space and time in our lives and a chance to just ponder and places like Earlshall Muir allow our mind to naturally drift and in doing so can bring a feeling of connection with the landscape. Take time here and see that it isn't empty or desolate or even remote at all. It just feels like it…and that's the beauty and value of it.

Ignore the first set of gates and go round a sharp bend to a second double gate that gives entry onto the Muir itself. Made up of very old sand dunes, the humps and bumps give a rougher walk. Crossing the wet flushes is made considerably easier by the boardwalks, great places to pause and hunt for dragonflies and damselflies.

The Muir can be buzzing with butterflies, birds and bees and it is a unique part of the path. Listen out for a lonely buzzard calling or watch out for the unmistakable flight of the marsh harrier.

The Muir slowly gives way, almost imperceptibly to the forest of Tentsmuir. Eventually the path leads out past beautiful wind-sculpted pine trees to a wooden gate onto a forest track. This is followed to meet the road leading to Tentsmuir Car Park. Turn east and follow this road past the Kinshaldy Stables, along Beech Avenue, through the vehicle barrier and onto the picnic area of the car park. This is a great place to halt and rest, the beach is just over the dunes and a toilet, playpark and information hub gives interest to a stop here.

Did You Know?
Eden Estuary

For most people, there's one place that can somehow sum up the essence of a particular part of the world capturing in a microcosm all that they love about the area. In Fife, for some this is one of the quaint fishing villages along the coastline of the East Neuk or it's the fun to be had on the beach at Burntisland and Aberdour or the historic splendour of St Andrews. For others it's the vast, unspoilt beauty of the Eden Estuary.

Set on the coastline to the north of St Andrews the Eden Estuary Local Nature Reserve lies side by side with the Tentsmuir National Nature Reserve and is summed up in three words – space, time and tide. For this is a place where the land meets the sea, and the space that blurs between the two is alive with wildlife and interest from the sandbanks and saltmarshes, to the dunes and mudflats.

The Eden Estuary is the third oldest local nature reserve in Scotland, having been declared a reserve in 1978. Its reserve status, along with its designation as a Site of Special Scientific Interest and a Special Protection Area, is in recognition of the environmental significance of the area and the wildlife that it hosts. Its long-standing status as a local nature reserve also ensures that facilities at the reserve are ideal for those who want to make the most of it and explore. The Eden Estuary Centre, within the village of Guardbridge, is at the heart of the reserve and offers a spectacular view, reserve information, toilet and parking.

Close by are the waymarked short walks of the Kincaple Den loop out of Guardbridge along the River Eden and back along the Fife Coastal Path running on the southern shore of the estuary, which are three kilometres in length. The short loop of Tip Point Trail out from the Motray Water to the north shore of the estuary is only 1.5 kilometres long, but what a nice wee walk seeing wildflowers, woodland and a big view.

And even the shortest walk around the estuary will confirm why it is famed

Keep your eyes peeled as you may see some goldfinches on your walk along the path

for its bird life, which draws many visitors to the area. The mudflats play host to wading birds and wildfowl and in particular, the area is noted for the arrival of the great winter flocks of waders such as black-tailed godwit, redshank and grey plover. Bird lovers will also be able to see great wildfowl too, shelducks, eider, goldeneye, wigeon and teal. Over the colder months, many different species of geese including brent, bean, barnacle and white-fronted will make the estuary their stopping off point.

Further up the banks of the estuary, where the river runs at a slower pace, look out for warblers and buntings in the summer reeds and the very good possibility of catching a glimpse of a kingfisher is an all year attraction from the Eden Centre.

And with peregrines, osprey and marsh harriers making regular appearances throughout the summer, it's easy to understand why the Eden Estuary captivates so many visitors.

Certainly the site should be on any birders hit list with recent sightings of lesser yellowlegs, sea eagle, little egret and great grey shrike adding a more exotic spin to the mass of more usual sightings. If migrants are your thing, drop in around spring and autumn.

To pass the Eden Estuary off as just another beautiful place to bird watch would be a mistake. The sandbanks towards the mouth of the estuary are an ideal place to see both harbour and grey seals whilst bottlenose dolphins and porpoises can be spotted playing off shore too. Even if the marine life isn't performing to a schedule matching yours, the views alone will be enough to make up for it. The reserve also plays host to otters, foxes, badger and brown hare. Bats are numerous around Guardbridge in the summer months too.

Inland, where the pace is a little more tranquil, wildflowers populate the dunes attracting butterflies such as comma and grayling as well as many bee species and, in turn, bird life. But, if the pace here seems a little sedate, nearby is Tentsmuir Forest which has a range of waymarked trails for biking or walking. Try linking the two sites and experience both sea and forest in a full day out under the watchful eyes of the forests resident roe deer and red squirrels.

Whatever you choose to do at the Eden Estuary though, it will certainly be memorable.

Tentsmuir Forest has waymarked trails for cycling and walking

LOCAL BUSINESSES

LEUCHARS

Accommodation

Hillpark House B&B, 96 Main Street, Leuchars, KY16 OHF. Tel: 01334 839280, enquiries@hillparkhouse.co.uk, www.hillparkhouse.com

Food and Beverage

Spar Convenience Store, 43-46 Main Street, Leuchars, KY16 OHE. Tel: 01334 839314, www.spar.co.uk

New Delight Takeaway, 18 Main Street, Leuchars, KY16 OHE. Tel: 01334 839942

The Golden Pagoda Takeaway, 49 Main Street, Leuchars. Tel: 01334 838528

Coach House Café, Main Street, Leuchars, KY16 OHF. Tel: 01334 870272

Aero Café, 10 Main Street, Leuchars, KY16 OHN. Tel: 01334 839285

Commercial Arms Pub, 60 Main Street, Leuchars, KY16 OHE. Tel: 01334 839284

Bank

ATM, Spar, 43-46 Main Street, Leuchars, KY16 OHE

Medical

Leuchar's Pharmacy, 14 Main Street, Leuchars, KY16 OHE. Tel: 01334 838 884

Other

Fife Cycle Centre, 2 Meadow Road, Leuchars, KY16 0EX. Tel: 01334 838989, www.fifecycles.co.uk

Tentsmuir to Tay Bridge

Tentsmuir Point

Tentsmuir Sands

Tentsmuir Point Nature Reserve

Tentsmuir Forest

Lundin Bridge

Tayport

01 **P**

02 **P**

Newport-on-Tay

B946

Tay Road Bridge

03 **P**

A92

A914

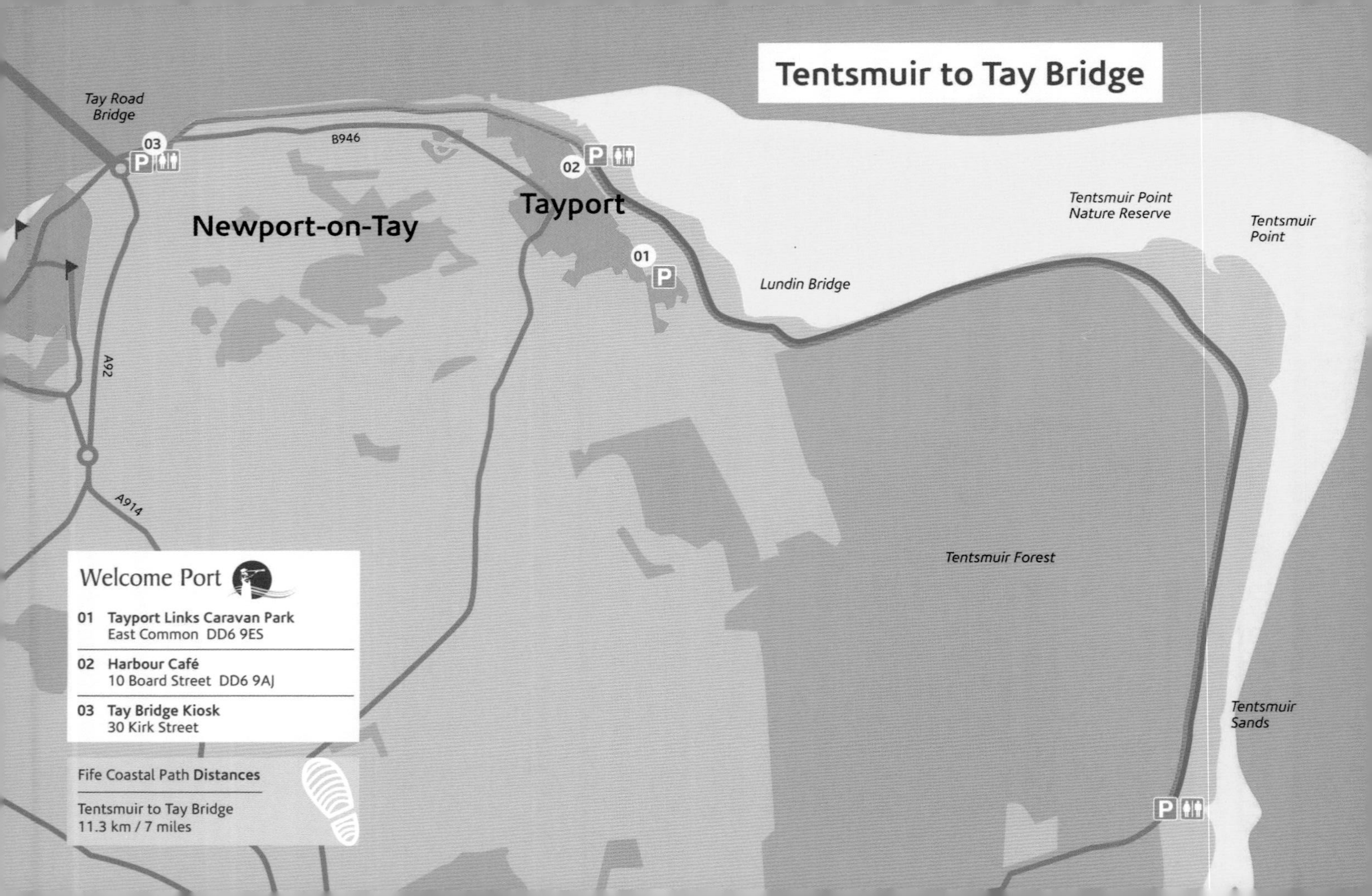

Welcome Port

01 Tayport Links Caravan Park
East Common DD6 9ES

02 Harbour Café
10 Board Street DD6 9AJ

03 Tay Bridge Kiosk
30 Kirk Street

Fife Coastal Path Distances

Tentsmuir to Tay Bridge
11.3 km / 7 miles

CHAPTER NINETEEN

TENTSMUIR TO THE TAY BRIDGE

THIS section of the Fife Coastal Path is 7 miles (10.5 km) long and takes you through the Tentsmuir Forest out across the Tayport Heath into Tayport. This section is on mainly good quality forest track giving easy walking underfoot and suitable for bikes and off-road pushchairs. From Tayport to the Tay Road Bridge is a tarmac surfaced high-level walk along the outer Tay Estuary with views north to Broughty Ferry and Dundee. Easy walking underfoot and good for cycles and off-road pushchairs. Start at the Tentsmuir Forest Car Park, which has a small charge by the Forestry Commission for parking.

Leaving the car park, head north through the large forestry gate on a wide forest road. Tentsmuir is the largest area of forestry in Fife, however it is relatively recent in origin. The forest was planted from the 1920s and before this time there was a vast area of dune heathland. This was and still is a rare and vulnerable habitat.

The remains of the dune heath can be seen clearly beneath the trees. The forest floor undulates with old sand dunes and hints at what this great heath must have looked like. The area is very dynamic and can lose or gain huge areas of land in a very short space of time. This coupled with locally strong off shore rips and currents make this a potentially dangerous, but interesting coastline.

Carry on through the forest and keep an eye out for red squirrels, a favourite haunt for these elusive and endangered tree dwellers. This is ideal habitat for them and Tentsmuir is one of their Fife strongholds. By the way, red squirrels don't hibernate nor do they live on acorns.

They love pinecones, dry their own fruit and mushrooms, can travel miles, be red, black and even appear grey, lose all their fur if stressed and go bonkers if you get too close.

They are very entertaining wee critters. You may not see them, but hunt the forest floor for their distinctive chewed cones. Roe deer, crossbill and woodpeckers can be seen along this stretch too, and in autumn keep an eye on the forest floor for interesting fungi.

A wee bit of care is necessary not to stray too far into the forest; it's incredibly easy to become disorientated and is also a stronghold of a less appealing creature, the tick.

Tentsmuir is at its best on a warm summer evening when the scent of pine mixes with the heat of the evening sun and the distant rhythmic wash of the sea induces a seriously peaceful feeling...watch out, nodding off isn't recommended just yet ...you still have a few miles to go!

The Icehouse was a subterranean building storing ice for salmon caught on the coast

The wide track finally leads to the Ice House. This subterranean structure was used to store ice for the salmon caught along this coast. Salmon were once in good numbers around the Tay mouth. This ice house is now home to bats and if passing on a summer evening walk, look out for their jerky acrobatic flight as they hoover up the midges...good fellows!

Keep to the coastal forest road straight on northwards until you begin a sharp left turning west. Here is a break in the trees and a great view is to be had if you care to pop through to the shore of the Tay.

Here you can watch the boats drift up and down the Tay. The great river is at your feet if the tide is in, so why not dip your toes into one of Britain's most interesting rivers. You know, more water flows down the Tay than any other river in the UK, in fact a greater volume than the Thames and the Severn combined.

The water at your feet may have fallen as rain on the summit of Ben Lawers, trickled off the peat into Loch Tay, flowed down the wide river past Dunkeld and Perth and gently joined the sea, passing Tentsmuir Point Nature Reserve and out across the Abertay Sands. The huge system of sandbars makes the Tay a hard place to navigate into, but a great place for grey seals.

A short walk east will reward you with a fantastic coastal view of these sandbars...and lots and lots of seals.

Continue west now for three kilometres to Tayport Heath. This is a great spot to rest up, take a seat on the benches and look over the saltmarsh for shelduck, eider and godwit.

A short walk west leads to Tayport itself, the northernmost habitation in Fife. Head for the caravan park, cutting straight through this and out on to Tayport Common. The view here is dominated by Broughty Ferry and in particular the castle. The path is a great spot on a windy day, here the sea wall is your only protection against the waves and walking too close can lead to a soaking, although it's great fun!

Tayport used to be a ferry port; in fact its original name was Ferryport-on-Craig. The ferries used to run across the Tay at the narrows between Tayport and Broughty Ferry. Alas, the road bridge put an end to that. Shame, the Tay is a lovely and lively stretch of water to be on.

Head towards the harbour and here you'll not find fishing vessels, but some lovely yachts. The harbour is privately owned and a friendly wee place. During the spring months watch out for the nesting mute swans. They have been nesting on the edge of the harbour for many years and indeed the locals have grown accustomed to them wandering around the village. Good amenities here, shops and a good loo.

From the harbour, follow the signs westward through some nice harbour fronts and onto the disused railway line. This is a tarmac cycleway and good for bikes, wheelchairs and pushchairs. This tarmac stretch leads all the way to the Tay Road Bridge.

The route passes close to the Tay shortly after leaving Tayport and there are some lovely wee spots to enjoy through the trees down by the river, great for fishing and picnicking. Along this stretch you can choose to take the 'high road' or the 'low road'. I recommend the low road along the shore leading past two fine wee lighthouses. These are private houses, but can easily be appreciated from the path.

A lovely stretch of mature woodland tells how long the railway has been closed. Look out for signs of the old railway and try to imagine this trip in the days of steam, chugging along the riverbank. Truly, a charming image.

The woodland gives way to open countryside with Dundee dominating the view now. This stretch slowly rises towards the Tay Road Bridge and marks the end of another good day walking on the Fife Coastal Path.

The Tay Road Bridge has little to inspire, except, if you wish a truly unusual view of the bridge and a sensational photo to act as a memento for completing this part of the Coastal Path. Head down along the road under the bridge, stand directly under the centre of the bridge and look towards the Dundee end. An optical illusion awaits that makes a striking image to end a great day.

The Tay Bridges link Fife with Tayside

Did You Know?
Red squirrels

The sight of a grey squirrel is a familiar one. From town parks to forest walks, and back gardens to playgrounds, these agile little creatures are commonly spotted streaking across the ground and up trees, or the occasional bold one ventures close enough to steal your picnic.

But, getting even a fleeting glimpse of a beautiful red squirrel is much more elusive and its survival is seriously under threat, largely as a result of its bold grey counterpart. The iconic red squirrel is Scotland's only native squirrel species and over recent years the population has declined significantly.

Only around 120,000 red squirrels are thought to remain in Scotland and what's more concerning is that this population is representative of around 75 per cent of the total UK population. Without serious and immediate intervention, this species could be lost to Scotland – and the rest of Britain – for ever.

Although red squirrel sightings were once commonplace throughout the UK, the introduction of the North American grey squirrel to England in the 19th century quickly and dramatically changed things.

The grey squirrel was introduced to English parkland by the Victorians who

The Fife Red Squirrel Project aims to protect this endangered species

were renowned for their love of bringing new, interesting and exotic species into the UK – Japanese knotweed is the most infamous – long before the risks of introducing non-native species were fully understood.

Within a very short period of time the grey squirrel had adapted to its new environment at the expense of the native reds as these creatures seem able to outrank the reds in almost all aspects essential to survival.

Physically bigger than reds, grey squirrels are also substantially more robust and can find and tolerate a wider range of food, giving them an easy advantage in finding and maintaining food sources and habitats. Their physical size also means they can compete and win with the reds in areas where food sources are scarcer. In addition, grey squirrels are carriers of the squirrelpox virus.

This highly contagious and virulent virus is lethal to red squirrels, but absolutely harmless to the grey squirrel. Add to this the grey squirrels more prolific and successful breeding habits and it's easy to understand why the march of the grey squirrels is seemingly unstoppable.

While the decline of the native red squirrel is due in the most part to the introduction of the grey squirrel, the loss of traditional habitats through the growth of infrastructure and changing land use practices have also played their part. The loss of traditional habitats just serves to increase the red squirrels' vulnerability to the stronger grey squirrel.

However, as can be said of many of our more vulnerable species, with awareness comes action. The red squirrel is identified as a priority species on the UK Biodiversity Action Plan and is also included on the Scottish Biodiversity List.

In parallel, the grey squirrel is identified on the UK Species Action List because of the role it plays in the decline of the reds. A dedicated project called 'Saving Scotland's Red Squirrels (SSRS)' was also set up in 2009.

This three-year project, a partnership between the Scottish Wildlife Trust, Scottish Natural Heritage, the Forestry Commission and Scottish Land and Estates, aims to 'halt the decline of red squirrel populations in key areas of north Scotland and improve habitat conditions to allow red squirrels to thrive and increase in number'.

Their work includes the surveying and monitoring of red squirrels and their habitats in Scotland, targeting grey squirrel control, particularly to prevent them gaining ground in key locations in the north of Scotland and also working to improve existing habitats for red squirrels. SSRS also provide information on where red squirrels can be spotted in Scotland.

In Fife, the Fife Red Squirrel Project – coordinated by the Fife Coast and Countryside Trust – concentrates its efforts on key sites for the species, as detailed in the Local Biodiversity Action Plan.

The Project also aims to raise awareness of red squirrels through work with schools and the coordination of information provision and advice. The work of the Project is also supported by a team of volunteers who get involved in the surveying and monitoring of red squirrels, as well as in the ever-important grey squirrel control. More information on all their work can be found at wwww.fiferedsquirrels.co.uk.

LOCAL BUSINESSES

TAYPORT

Accommodation

Elliot Cottage B&B, 30 William Street, Tayport, DD6 9HN.
Tel: 01382 553234

Tayport Links Caravan Park, East Common, Tayport, DD6 9ES.
Tel:01382 552 334,
Email: info@tayportlinkscaravanpark.co.uk
www.tayportlinkscaravanpark.co.uk

Food and Beverage

Harbour Café, 10 Board Street, Tayport, DD6 9AJ. Tel: 01382 553757

TAYPORT BRIDGE

Food and Beverage

Tay Bridge Kiosk, 30 Kirk Street, Tay Bridge, Fife. Tel: 01382 612469

Tay Bridge to Wormit Bay

Newport-on-Tay

Wormit

Woodhaven Pier

Tay Road Bridge

Tay Rail Bridge

A92

B945

B946

B946

01

02

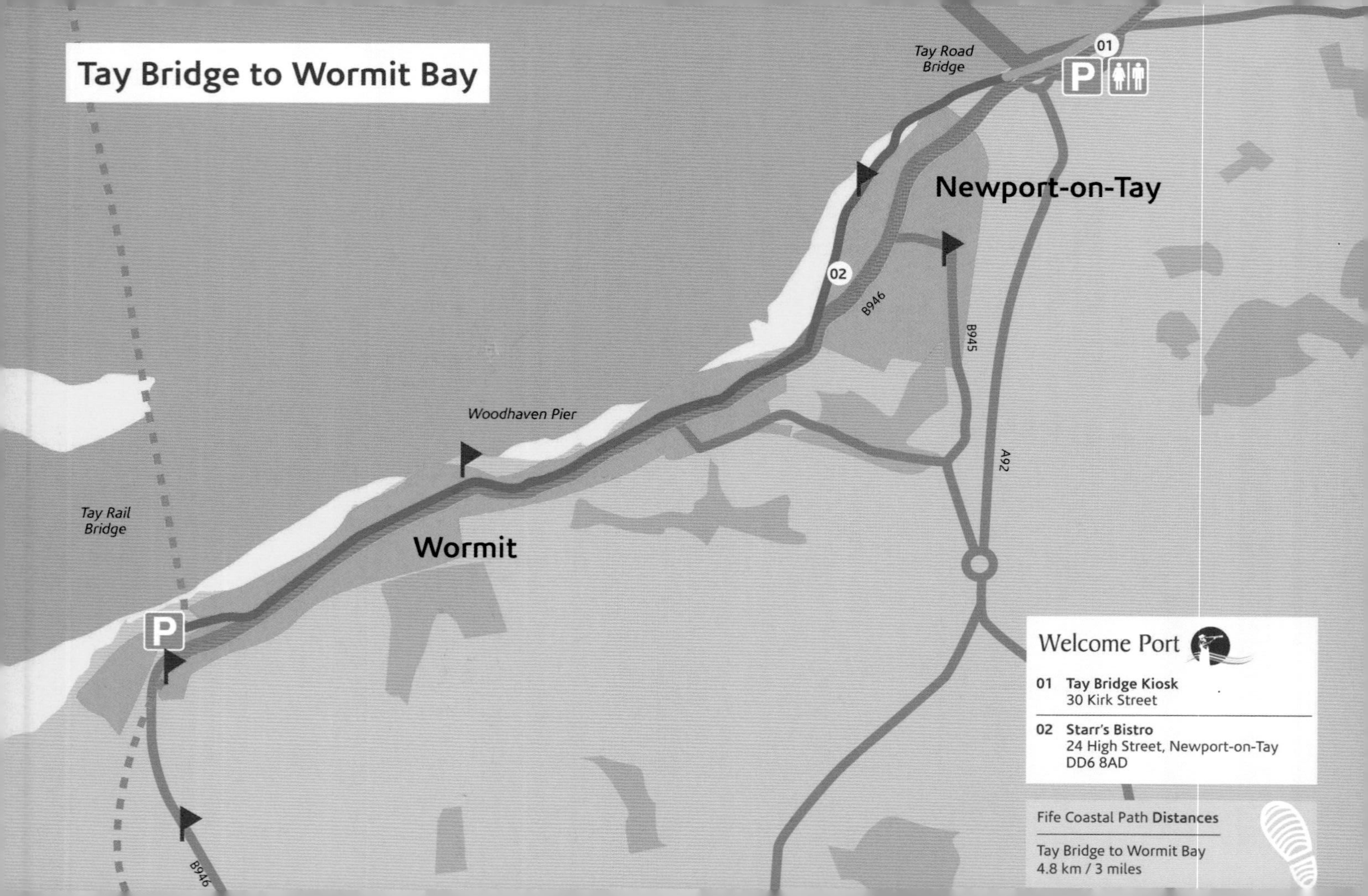

Welcome Port

01 **Tay Bridge Kiosk**
    30 Kirk Street

02 **Starr's Bistro**
    24 High Street, Newport-on-Tay
    DD6 8AD

Fife Coastal Path Distances

Tay Bridge to Wormit Bay
4.8 km / 3 miles

CHAPTER TWENTY

THE TAY BRIDGE TO WORMIT BAY

ORIGINALLY trained as a botanist, I became a Countryside Ranger really by accident after working in agriculture and adult education. After years driving family and friends to distraction every time we went out for a walk pointing out flora, fauna, tracks and signs, I trained in Conservation and Countryside Management at Elmwood College, Cupar, Fife as did many of my colleagues. I've been a Ranger for nearly ten years now and love every minute – although it is more of a lifestyle than a job.

Countryside Ranger
Kate Morison

The area I cover is Newport-on-Tay to Newburgh and south to the Howe of Fife. This area is quite different to the rest of Fife in geology and landscape character. It is quite rugged and hilly and used mostly for cattle farming, shooting and forestry. The views from along the North Fife Ridge are really spectacular.

The River Tay is the single most significant feature of the area. It is home to the biggest reed bed in the UK and a host of internationally important wildlife including marsh harriers, ospreys, bearded tits and more recently, sea eagles. Grey seals often venture up the Tay even as far as Newburgh and I see regular signs of otter, although I've yet to see one at close quarters.

This Section of Path is 3 miles (5 Km) and is easy walking along pavements. Start at Tay Bridgehead Car Park.

The northern extension is the last piece of the jigsaw in terms of completing the Fife Coastal Path. It's a challenging and fairly remote section, but well worth the effort. I look forward to seeing other people enjoy it as much as I do.

This section of the path runs along the sparsely populated North Coast of Fife. The landscape and resulting land use in this part of Fife are quite different from the rest of Fife. The magnificent River Tay and the Volcanic Ridge, which runs alongside the river, dominate views. This ridge forms part of the longer rampart of the Ochil Hills, which starts near Stirling and finally peters out at Newport.

This ridge was formed during the Devonian period 350-300 million years ago when Scotland was semi-arid, warm and situated south of the equator.

The River Tay is the longest river in Scotland and the largest volume river in the UK. It has a length of 193 kilometres – stretching from the slopes of Ben Lui to the Firth of Tay and has a catchment area in excess of 5,000 square kilometres. The North Coast is steeped in history with Iron Age hill forts, ruined Abbeys and stately piles. This is a long stretch taken in its entirety and would constitute a full day walking for a fairly fit walker. This is an ideal winter walk for the dedicated walker when the weather won't allow a trip further north.

For the less energetic, each section has its own unique charm and it may be more enjoyable to experience the route in sections over several visits.

From Tay Bridgehead, where you can get a very reasonably priced cup of tea and bacon roll, the path passes under the Tay Road Bridge. As a student I cycled to Dundee from Newport regularly and I can confirm that the bridge is higher on the Newport side of the river.

The road bridge was opened in 1966 at a cost of £4.8m. This was cheap compared

The Tayport Bandstand overlooking the River Tay

with the estimated £400m for the new Forth crossing. When the bridge first opened 6500 vehicles a day used it. Now the daily crossing volume is around 250,000 vehicles – that's roughly a 40-fold increase in around 40 years.

Now, continue west along the riverside road. Newport-on-Tay was originally known as 'new Dundee' and as the name suggests it developed as a *des res* area for the wealthy jute barons of Dundee. Newport has long been a focus for crossing the river from Fife to Dundee with no fewer than three piers. As you walk along, it's hard not to be impressed by the sheer scale and grandeur of some of the Victorian houses overlooking the river. Look out for a cast iron mile marker made in 1824 in Kirkcaldy as part of the 'Great Fife Road'. This road ran

This cast iron mile marker was made in 1842 for the Great Fife Road

from Pettycur Bay in the south of Fife via staging posts at New Inn and Cupar.

You will pass on your right a recently restored Victorian drinking fountain on the riverside braes, once a popular picnic spot and still a good place to stop and get your sandwiches out on a sunny day. You may even spot a sandwich tern flying up the river. You will soon pass along Newport Main Street.

Take the road which follows the river and you will come to the old steamboat station and harbour built by the illustrious Scots engineer, Thomas Telford, in 1823. This must have been a bustling place in its heyday with the well-heeled Dundee merchant society travelling to and fro across the river.

THE FIFE COASTAL PATH

Continue along the route past Woodhaven pier where Norwegian 'flying boats' were stationed during WWII and on through Wormit. The people of Wormit claimed to be the first Scottish village to have installed domestic electricity. A windmill located on Wormit Hill generated the power, with a steam engine supplementing this when the wind was low. A coal-gas engine later replaced this until the 1930s, when Wormit was connected to the national grid. Alexander Stewart, who built many of the houses in Wormit, offered electrical lighting to homeowners and also basic street lighting. Consumers paid ten shillings a quarter and could use as much electricity as they liked.

The first houses to have electricity had sun rays painted on the front as a symbol that they were the first, and this is mostly noticeable along the highest row of terraced housing in the village, on Hill Crescent.

The name Wormit comes from the Norwegian word 'orme' meaning serpent. As to why Wormit was named after a serpent I don't know. Possibly after the eels that periodically run up the river?

Take a right turn along Bay Road, which passes under the Tay Rail Bridge. The 2-mile (3.5 km) long Tay Rail Bridge, designed by W.H. Barlow & Sons opened in 1887 to replace the earlier bridge of Thomas Bouch, which collapsed in 1879 on a stormy December night , a year after its completion. All 75 of the passengers on a train that was crossing perished in the river below. You can still see the foundations of the original bridge sticking up out of the water. Coincidentally, one of the oldest pear trees in Fife – a Lindores pear also blew down that same night just outside Newburgh – more on that story later. Carry on along Bay Road, admiring the view up the Tay as you go to Wormit Bay.

Did You Know?
Tay Bridges and the Tay Bridge Disaster

The night of December 28, 1879 marks one of the bleakest moments in Fife's long history. At just after 7pm, the catastrophic collapse of the Tay Rail Bridge plunged a six-carriage train travelling from Edinburgh into the icy waters of the Firth of Tay and resulted in the deaths of all 75 people on board.

For the families of the victims and the country at large, the shock at how this could have happened, just months after the bridge had opened and been declared safe, was immense. But, the questions the disaster asked of a burgeoning engineering industry, and those who placed their faith in it, loomed just as large.

Plans to span the breadth of the Firth of Tay and connect the city of Dundee with Fife, just over two miles away, date back as far as the 1850s, but work on the Tay Bridge began in earnest some 20 years later, under the watch of engineer Thomas Bouch.

Tay Bridgehead where you can get a refreshing cuppa!

Originally from Cumbria, Thomas Bouch had established a strong reputation as a railway engineer north of the border, designing parts of Waverley Station, in Edinburgh and railways in Fife, before undertaking the design of the Tay Bridge.

Work began on the bridge in 1871 and it was officially opened on 1st June, 1878 with Thomas Bouch receiving a Knighthood shortly after. At its opening, the bridge was the longest in the world, receiving international recognition as a feat of engineering and a triumph of man over nature.

However, what was lesser known was that the construction of the bridge had been fraught with difficulties, from inexperienced workers to unforeseen problems in the geology of the riverbed and hasty redesigns and girder collapses during construction.

After an official inquiry into the disaster, followed by years of academic investigation, it is most widely concluded that a combination of poor design, poor workmanship and high winds caused the fateful collapse of December 1879.

The public inquiry into the collapse of the bridge was damning in its condemnation of Bouch concluding that: 'For these defects both in the design, the construction, and the maintenance, Sir Thomas Bouch is, in our opinion, mainly to blame.'

The results of the inquiry marked the end of Bouch's career and reputation

Wormit Bay

and the opportunity to design the Forth Rail Bridge, a job for which he had already been selected. Bouch died, at the age of 58, shortly after the inquiry drew its conclusions.

Although blame had been swiftly apportioned, the legacy of the disaster loomed large in minds for years to come, with the famous Scottish poet, William McGonagall going so far as to pen a verse in its memory in 1880.

Having seen a little of the potential that a rail link between Fife and Dundee could bring, work soon began on a new, safer, replacement. Experienced railway engineer William Henry Barlow – who had sat on the inquiry panel into the Tay Bridge Disaster – designed the bridge with his son Crawford Barlow working alongside.

Work on the new bridge began in 1883 and opened, parallel to the site of the original bridge, four years later in 1887. Although substantial refurbishments have been undertaken over the years – the most recent being a multi-million pound project in 2003 which included the removal of hundreds of tonnes of bird droppings and the replacement of rivets and bolts – the bridge remains in use to this day.

In 1966 the trip between Dundee and Fife was made even easier with the opening of the Tay Road Bridge. Totalling 2,250 metres in length, the bridge took three years to build and is constructed of 42 spans supported by concrete piers across the breadth of the river. The bridge employs 36 staff, ensuring that this main artery between Fife and Tayside runs smoothly for the thousands of commuters who use it every week.

For the most up-to-date information on the road bridge visit http://www.tayroadbridge.co.uk.

LOCAL BUSINESSES

NEWPORT ON TAY

Accommodation

Oakbank B&B, Wester Kinnear, Newport on Tay, DD6 8RH.
Tel: 01382 330069,
linda@oakbankb-b.co.uk,
www.oakbankb-b.co.uk

Food and Beverage

Starr's Coffee Shop, 24 High Street, Newport on Tay, DD6 8AD.
Tel: 01382 540066,
ask@starrs-newport.co.uk ,
www.starrs-newport.co.uk

Brig O Tay Tavern, 14 Boat Road, Newport on Tay, DD6 8EZ.
Tel: 01382 541274

Spar Convenience Store, 16 High Street, Newport on Tay. DD6 8AD.
Tel: 01382 543148

Scotmid Convenience Store, 48 High Street, Newport on Tay, DD6 8AD.
Tel: 01382 543172,
www.scotmid.co.uk

Wing Wah Chinese, 1 Boat Brae, Newport on Tay, DD6 8EX.
Tel: 01382 542683

The Silvery Tay, 54 High Street, Newport on Tay, DD6 8AD.
Tel: 01382 540300

Co-op Convenience Store, 46-50 High Street, Newport on Tay, DD6 8AD.
Tel: 01382 543172

Bank

ATM, 40 High Street, Newport on Tay, DD6 8AD

Post Office

Newport Post Office, 19 Cupar Road, Newport on Tay, DD6 8AF.
Tel: 01383 543170

Medical

Rowland Pharmacy, 16 Victoria Street, Newport on Tay, DD6 8DJ.
Tel: 01382 543179

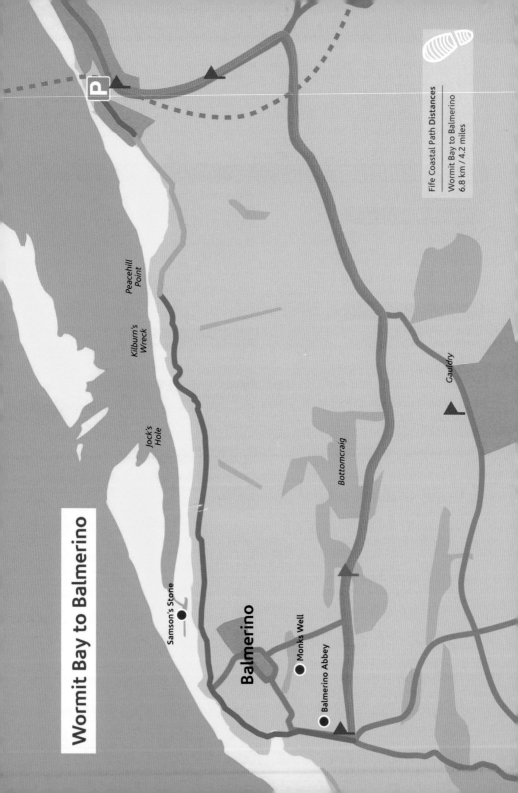

Wormit Bay to Balmerino

Peacehill Point

Kilburn's Wreck

Jock's Hole

Samson's Stone

Balmerino

Monks Well

Balmerino Abbey

Bottomcraig

Gauldry

Fife Coastal Path Distances

Wormit Bay to Balmerino
6.8 km / 4.2 miles

CHAPTER TWENTY ONE

WORMIT BAY TO BALMERINO

THIS section, which starts at Wormit Bay Car Park, is 4.2 miles (2.6 km) and some of the path is stepped and steep. Most of the path is unsurfaced.

The path around the bay has been resurfaced to allow multi-use access to Peacehill Point. From here to Nether Kirkton the path is unsurfaced, steep and stepped in places. To download leaflets for this section of path visit the publications section of the Fife Coastal Path website: www.fifecoastandcountrysidetrust.co.uk.

Walking round Wormit Bay you might notice some rocks in the path that look as though they might be made of iron. These are remnants of the Iron Foundry that was sited here to produce iron for the bridges.

You may also notice people raking over the beach with their eyes fixed firmly on the ground. Most likely they will be looking for agates – semi-precious stones that look like old potatoes until opened to reveal the gems inside.

In fact, the Wormit Balmerino shore is designated a SSSI (Site of Special Scientific Interest) on account of its geology providing the most completely exposed section in Fife through the Lower Devonian lavas that form the Ochil Hills and associated sedimentary rocks of Fife. These rocks are of international importance for the information they give about the geography of Southern Scotland at that time.

The Tay Estuary supports nationally and internationally important wildfowl and wader populations and when the tide goes back at Wormit Bay to expose the mudflats, you will often see birds feeding here.

The Tay Estuary mud is full of tiny creatures – shrimps, snails, worms and young flatfish – great food for birds. Groups of curlew are common as are redshank and oystercatcher and you may see brightly coloured shelduck pootling about on the mud.

Looking along the river towards Perth you should be able to make out the remains of a fishing station. Salmon fishing was a major industry on the Tay for hundreds of years and these bothies are common all the way up the river to Perth. Men would come here from as far away as Stornoway for the fishing season to live in overcrowded and very basic accommodation – often the only furniture would be made from fish boxes.

At the far end of the bay is Peacehill Point; a great place to look back along the river at the bridges. You might want to take a seat on the Common Seal bench.

There is a population of several hundred seals in the Tay Estuary – common and grey. Numbers have declined sharply in the last 20 years possibly due to

Above is one of the seal sculptures between Wormit and Balmerino and left is the Kilburn Wreck

disease, a drop in fish numbers or injuries from water vessels. The common seal population in the Tay Estuary represents more than one per cent of the European population. These lovely creatures are quite curious and I have been lucky enough to canoe down the Tay to be surrounded by seals on the approach to the rail bridge. The seals like to haul out on the sandbanks that appear in the estuary at low tide, often just looking like banana-shaped blobs.

There are three new seal sculptures on the path between Wormit and Balmerino put there to sit on and to see what a seal looks like close up. Look out for them as you follow the path.

From Wormit Bay the path follows the Right of Way along the coast and becomes unsurfaced, steep and stepped in places. Soon you will pass through a gate into some fields, which may have sheep and cattle in them at times.

Woods between the fields and the shore hold some fairly old ash and oak trees and bluebell, which would suggest that there have been woods here for quite some time. Follow the path through these fields until you come to a second gate into an area called Jock's Hole.

If you look down to the shore from here in winter when the leaves are off the trees, you may be able to see the Kilburn Wreck, also called the Dunoon Boat. It lies about 300 yards offshore just west of Jock's Hole. The wreck was a converted steel barge built around 1940 in the USA. It was subsequently bought by the salvage company based at Kilburn Farm and was used in the 1980s to salvage metal from HMS Argyll, wrecked on the Bell Rock in 1915. Once the salvage was complete the barge was moored here and sank as a result of ice damage.

Follow the waymarked route past the old quarry and down the slope to a wooden bridge crossing the burn at the bottom of Jock's Hole – a lovely secluded

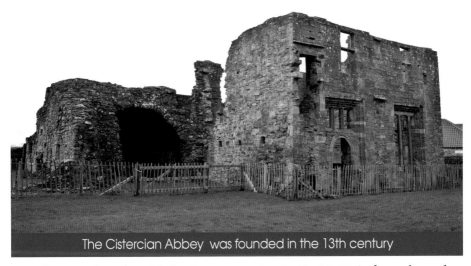

The Cistercian Abbey was founded in the 13th century

spot. Steps on the other side lead you up and out of Jock's Hole through another gate. From here the path carries on along the edge of an arable field where you might see 'Mad March Hares' in the springtime.

From the field you will pass into a long stretch of young woodland planted in the 1990s, or thereabouts, rising uphill to your left with the ancient woodland strip overhanging the path on your right. As the young forest has moved in, so has the wildlife associated with it. I often come across roe deer in these woods and the whole area bustles with birds. You may hear the drumming of the great spotted woodpecker or the 'teacher-teacher' of the great tit or the 'Tommy Gun' sound of the wren.

In the winter, many of the small birds come together in feeding flocks for safety from predators such as sparrowhawks. It is harder for the small birds to hide in the winter and many pairs of eyes are a distinct advantage. It is not unusual to find great tits, long-tailed tits, blue tits, coal tits, chaffinches and goldfinches all flying together. Siskins are fairly common here too and fly around in great restless swarms a bit like swarms of midges. If you're keen on foraging for wild food this stretch of the path is great for collecting sloes. There are also a couple of really prolific old cherry trees, but I don't want to give too much away.

In due course you will come to a fork in the path. The stump of an old beech tree is here. Sadly, the top part of the tree had to be removed as it was rotten and could have fallen onto the path at any time. Rather than remove the whole tree the stump has been left intentionally as an ideal home for bats and snack bar for woodpeckers that will come to feed on the beetle grubs in the dead wood.

The right hand fork nearest the river is the original route, which is becoming dangerous due to erosion, so take the left hand fork along the newly cleared path. Follow this path until you come to a field. Turn right here and follow the steps down to rejoin the riverside path. After heading west along this path for a short way you will emerge from the trees at Nether Kirkton.

Nether Kirkton was once a major salmon fishing station. A report from 1846 describes salmon-fishing being carried out on the Tay with 'encouraging success' with 'the whole of the fisheries on the river affording employment to nearly 500 men; the annual number of fish taken is 25,000 salmon and 50,000 grilse most of which are shipped to London by the Dundee steamers, which perform the voyage in about 35 hours.'

The salmon were caught using coble boats and nets, a process which I can remember watching with fascination as a child at the mouth of the Tweed where some of my uncles were salmon fishermen. It wasn't uncommon for 30 or 40 big fish to be landed from a single cast – some of the fish as big as me.

Continue on the path between the house and the shore and head towards Balmerino. Just beyond Nether Kirkton a large round boulder lies on the shore. This boulder is of a different type of rock to the rocks found locally and is known as Samson's Stone. How did it get here?

The explanation is that the glacier ice at the end of the last Ice Age deposited it here some 10,000 years ago (A more fun explanation is that it was thrown here by the giant who lived at the top of Norman's Law who was aiming at the giant who lived at the top of Dundee Law but missed.)

The next house you pass on your left is another old fishing bothy that has been converted into a house. Continue along the path until you come to the third seal sculpture at a small point overlooking the bay at Balmerino.

If you look towards Perth you will see Flisk Woods bordering the shore heading into the distance. Closer to hand are the remains of Balmerino Pier, which was once a bustling port handling mainly grain and potatoes and landing coal.

Most of the locals were employed in the salmon fishery, or as weavers doing piecework from home. In the nineteenth century the village of Balmerino was a popular holiday destination. Pleasure steamers carried day-trippers from Dundee to enjoy Balmerino and nearby Newburgh. Balmerino is one of the best places I know to enjoy a sunset on a summer's evening – just superb and something difficult to describe in words.

At this point the path heads inland and passes the ancient Cistercian Abbey founded in the 13th century by King Alexander II and his mother Queen Ermengarde. The monks came from Melrose Abbey, in the Scottish Borders. In all probability, the monks would have brought fruit trees with them as they did at Newburgh and quite a few fruit trees still grow in odd corners of the gardens around the Abbey today.

The grounds of the Abbey are home to a wonderful old sweet chestnut tree, probably planted in the 16th century and certainly one of the oldest in Britain. Did Mary Queen of Scots plant it? There is a record of Mary visiting the Abbey in 1565, so theoretically it is a possibility and a good story too.

LOCAL BUSINESSES

WORMIT

Food and Beverage

The View, Naughton Road, Wormit, DD6 8NE. Tel: 01382 542579

Wormit Stores, 1 Mount Stuart Road, Wormit, DD6 8NH.
Tel: 01382 541638

Post Office

Wormit Post Office, 3 Naughton Road, Wormit, DD6 8NE.

Tel: 01382 541724

Balmerino to Newburgh

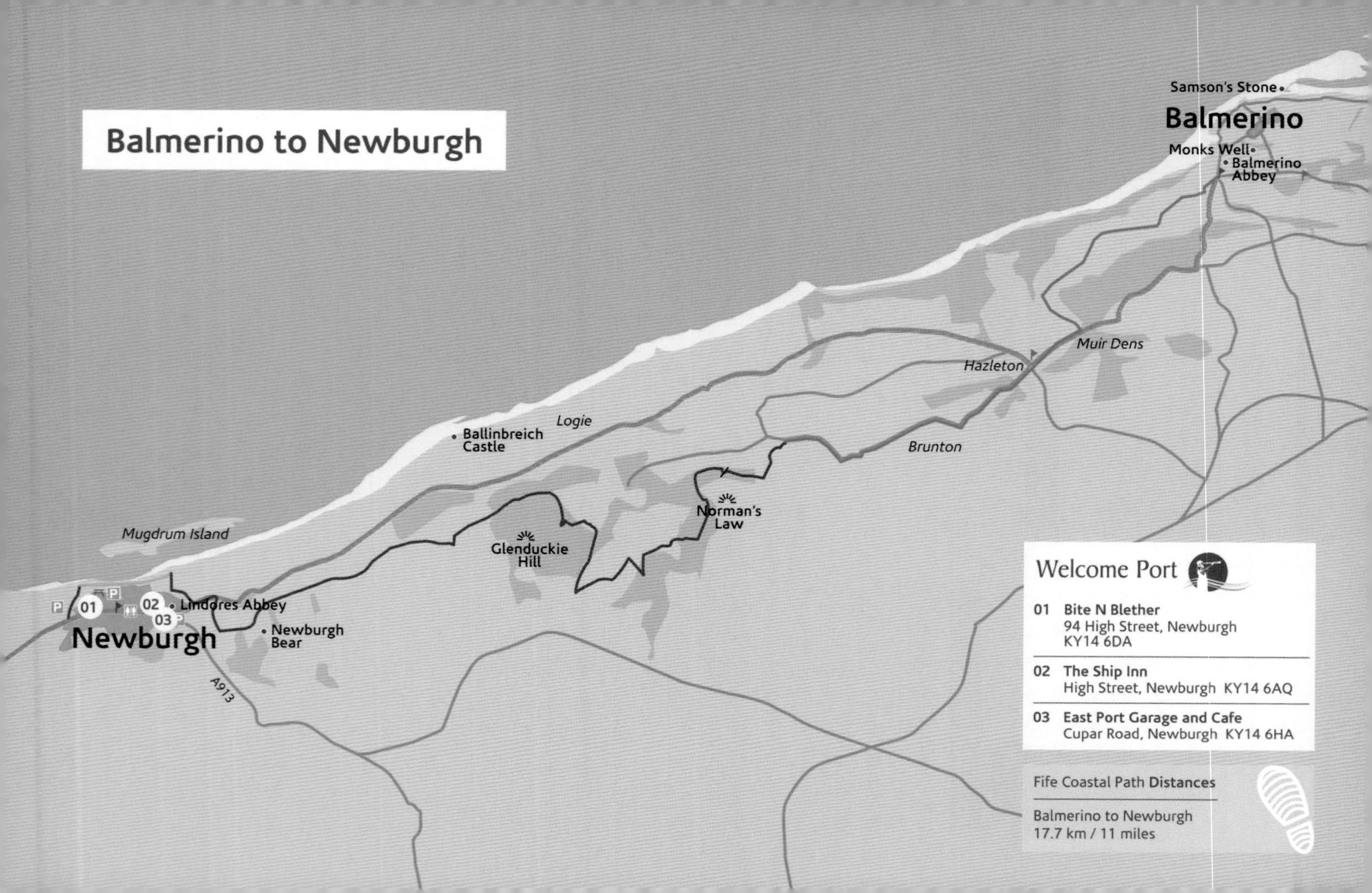

Samson's Stone

Balmerino

Monks Well
• Balmerino
  Abbey

Muir Dens

Hazleton

Brunton

Norman's
Law

Logie

Glenduckie
Hill

Ballinbreich
Castle

Mugdrum Island

Lindores Abbey

• Newburgh
  Bear

Newburgh

A913

Welcome Port

01 Bite N Blether
    94 High Street, Newburgh
    KY14 6DA

02 The Ship Inn
    High Street, Newburgh KY14 6AQ

03 East Port Garage and Cafe
    Cupar Road, Newburgh KY14 6HA

Fife Coastal Path Distances

Balmerino to Newburgh
17.7 km / 11 miles

CHAPTER TWENTY TWO

BALMERINO TO NEWBURGH

THIS is an 11-mile (17.5 km) section on roads and unmade track, steep and remote for much of its length. Start at Balmerino Abbey where you can park at the roadside. There are also some optional loops offering circular walks off this section of the Coastal Path. (Details at the end of this chapter.)

Follow the route uphill and through a gap in the hedge to pass round the white cottages and head west along a lovely old farm road. The hedgerows along this track are stunning in the spring and early summer as they are packed with Jack-by-the-hedge, red campion and cow parsley amongst other wildflowers and alive with insects and small songbirds.

Listen out for the yellowhammer and his 'a-little-bit-of-bread-and-no-cheeese' song. If you look down to the coast while walking along the path you may see Birkhill Castle peeping out from among the trees. This is the home of Lord and Lady Dundee, who own Birkhill Estate, which takes in most of the land in this area. The estate is managed for farming, forestry and shooting and is fairly typical of the land use in this part of Fife.

The track carries on past Thornton to Home Farm before heading uphill to join with the coast road at Muirdens. Take a right here and follow the road over the crossroads and along towards Creich, enjoying the views of Norman's Law as you go. You will pass the ruins of Creich Castle on your left. There's been a castle on this site since at least the 13th century (However the present building is thought to date to the first half of the 16th century, as it is mentioned in a charter of 1553.)

On your right are the ruins of Old Creich Church, also dated from the 13th century and which was superseded by the new parish church about a mile away just outside Luthrie in 1832. The new church contains a stone with medieval carvings from the original. The grounds of the old church contain a fine old yew tree. Yews are known for their longevity – the ancient yew at Fortingall is now estimated to be around 5,000 years old and probably the oldest living thing in Europe. As a tree whose possible life outspans that of all other trees as well as much of human history to date, the yew is symbolic of the sum of all wisdom.

The yew is said to guard the doorway between this life and the next. As a sacred tree of immortality from pagan times, the yew is associated with burial places where it was believed to protect and purify the dead. The custom of putting sprigs of yew inside the shrouds of the dead was similarly believed to protect the soul on its journey through the underworld.

Moving swiftly on, the path takes up past the small village of Brunton and onwards to Norman's Law. People have lived in this part of the world for thousands of years. There are the remains of Iron Age hillforts and hut circles right along the North Fife Ridge, on Norman's Law, Glenduckie Hill, Green Hill by Coultra, Drumnod by Creich and Castle Law.

A Bronze Age log boat was discovered at Carpow near the mouth of the River Earn. (It was made from a single piece of oak carbon-dated back to the Bronze Age). Carpow was also the location for a massive Roman camp when Septimius Severus headed north to fight the locals in AD209, sailing up the Tay and landing some 20,000 men here.

The thing that I find most striking about North Fife is how depopulated and quiet it has become in the space of less than 100 years. The Tay would have been busy with all kinds of cargo and pleasure boats calling in at the various harbours and fishing stations. The villages would have been lively with people working on the land and walking from one place to another. At one time the school in Flisk had a roll of 80 children. The school closed in 1981 and the school at Luthrie closed more recently. How times change.

Just beyond Pittachope Farm, pronounced Pichope, the path leaves the road and heads up toward Norman's Law. Follow the track uphill into woodland, following the forest track. At the top of the slope look out for a stile on your left. Should you want to take in the view from the top of Norman's Law as part of your walk, this is the most direct way to get to it. From the top there are fantastic views of Fife and beyond and a helpful viewfinder to identify the hilltops.

The North Fife hills are home to some fairly unusual lichen-rich heaths worth looking at, and which have a kind of moonscape feel. The heaths are home to the green hairstreak butterfly, a fairly uncommon species that only flies on warm sunny days in May, so that opportunities for seeing it are limited.

The path continues through conifer woods for some distance to finally emerge at some cottages above Ayton. Here the path doubles back on itself to take you past the cottages into a track running through trees and left down a field edge towards Glenduckie Hill.

Follow the signage to take you back up round the east side of the hill to a small parking area where you will find a makeshift seat overlooking a pond. I have found this to be a great location for spotting birds of prey, once seeing sea eagles, buzzards, a sparrowhawk, a kestrel and a peregrine in the space of half an hour. It's worth stopping here for a while to see what appears in the sky.

Since 2007 the RSPB have been carrying out a release programme of sea eagles, which were once native to the UK. Chicks are brought from Norway each spring and held in pens at a site near here until they are released around

The Tay Reed Beds are an important habitat for wildlife

August. All the birds are fitted with wing-tags and radio backpacks so that they can be tracked. The project will run for five years and see the release of around 70 birds. (Look up the RSPB blog for more details). The birds have established a roosting site close by and are now regularly seen over the Tay. They can have a massive eight-feet wingspan, so are quite easy to spot. They don't get their distinctive white tail feathers until they are five years old, so still look a bit like oversized buzzards with square-ended wings.

Follow the track, which takes you round the northern face of Glenduckie Hill and then veers off through young woodland to emerge at the top of a narrow, arable field. Look out for short-eared owls searching for voles in the long grass as you pass through the young woodland. The path continues along the top edge of a field then through a fenced section between cow fields at the top of Higham Hill. This is quite a steady climb but the path soon starts to head back towards the coast and downhill towards Newburgh through a strip of pine trees known as Blinkie Strip.

Emerging from Blinkie Strip you will get a good viewpoint over the estuary and an appreciation of the extent of the Tay reed beds. These are the largest reed beds in the UK covering over 2000 acres. They were planted in the late 18th century, at least partly by prisoners from the Napoleonic War, to stop the Tay's banks eroding and to protect reclaimed land such as the flat strip of land you see below you extending along to Newburgh.

At one time the reeds were harvested and sold as thatching material. A

Above is Lindores Abbey, which is arguably the birthplace of Scottish whisky and below, the old water wheel at the side of the Mill House

thatched roof of wheat will last only 15 to 20 years, whereas reeds will last 80 to 100 years. Reeds also capture carbon while growing and are a renewable resource making them incredibly environmentally friendly – maybe reed thatch will become commercially viable again in years to come.

Reed beds are incredibly rich in insect life, holding more recorded insect species than even an oak tree and they are also an important habitat for some of our more specialist wildlife, such as marsh harrier and bearded tit. As you might expect, reed buntings, or `vicar of the reeds' thrive here and in the summer you will often hear the rasping sound of the elusive sedge warbler. The reed beds are a valuable roosting site for swallows and martins in the summer and flocks of starlings in the winter.

When the tide is low, the many and extensive sand and mudbanks are exposed. These have great names such as Carthagena Bank, Peesweep Bank and Sure as Death Bank. The plants and small animals on these banks provide valuable feeding grounds for wildfowl and wading birds and offer safe roosts.

In the winter the estuary is home to thousands of birds, mostly pink-footed geese and ducks such as teal and wigeon. Wildfowling is still very much part of the local culture in Newburgh and you will often see men and dogs in tiny boats heading bravely out into the estuary in the cold and damp over the winter months.

Follow the path on a gentle incline downhill towards Newburgh. To your right is the site of the Battle of Blackearnside, where William Wallace defeated the Earl of Pembroke in 1298. Go through the two self-closing gates near the bottom of the hill and follow the path round the field edges to come out at a pond opposite Parkhill steading. Look for the old water wheel at the side of the Mill House, which has recently been restored.

Walk along the pavement toward Newburgh and you will soon come to the ruins of Lindores Abbey. David, Earl of Huntingdon, brother of William the Lion, is thought to have founded the abbey as a daughter house of Kelso Abbey, about 1191.

If you turn and look back at the hill you have come down you should be able to see the outline of the Newburgh Bear. The bear is only a few years old and was cut for a local community project in 1980. A worker from Parkhill Farm ploughed the outline. The bear is believed to be a depiction of a stone called the Bear Stone, from which the Bear Tavern takes its name. It was originally set into the abbot's residence at Lindores Abbey. The bear and ragged staff is the symbol of the Earls of Warwick, and as a crozier, or pastoral staff, is evident above the now obliterated arms of Warwick, it may be assumed that the stone was caused to be made by Guy, the first Abbot, who was a cadet – the brother or son – of that family.

Lindores Abbey is arguably the birthplace of Scottish whisky, as the earliest record of whisky is a 1494 commission from King James IV to Friar John Cor of Lindores Abbey to make about 580 kg of aquavitae. Too late for William Wallace, unfortunately, as it would have been a fitting toast to his victory along the road.

Newburgh was made a Royal Burgh by Charles I in the 15th century. It is renowned for its orchards, having more fruit trees in its gardens than any other town in Scotland.

The monks would have brought trees with them when the Abbey was established and as late as the 1800s there was an orchard of apples and pears beside the Abbey of some eight acres. Some of the pear trees were unique to the area dating back to before the Reformation. Sadly, the largest of these trees blew down on the night of the Tay Rail Bridge disaster on December 28, 1879. It was a massive tree with a trunk measuring 18 feet in girth. It is thought that only one Lindores pear tree survives. However, Newburgh still has a thriving orchard group who hold fruit sales on the High Street, from August to October (www. newburghorchards.org.uk).

Interest in orchard fruit has seen a resurgence in recent years, so hopefully the community will now be able to get support to conserve and restore their ancient fruit heritage.

From Lindores Abbey follow the path alongside the road to Scotland Terrace. Turn right into Scotland Terrace then right again onto a track called Kitty's Goat, which leads you through fields back to the riverbank. Turn left here and follow the path past the sailing club.

In addition to salmon fishing, Newburgh is home to one of only three spawning grounds of the sparling or smelt (*Osmerus eperlanus*). This fish, a smaller relative of the salmon, used to be caught in great quantities at Newburgh using fixed stake nets and was much valued by the local inhabitants, many of whom would not be able to afford salmon. The smelt apparently has a cucumber taste.

Its population and ecology in the Tay is still poorly understood. Smelt use gravel beds at the limit of the tidal reach of rivers in which to spawn, the prime time being the first full moon in March. A study has been carried out in recent years to precisely locate the spawning grounds and look at the feasibility of fishing commercially for smelt. Currently only a few boats fish for smelt on a small scale between September and early March.

Continuing along the river you will come to a series of four piers jutting out into the river. Opposite is Mugdrum Island, which divides the river into two channels the North and South Deep.

Newburgh was once a busy port exporting linen made in the town and surrounding villages to the West Indies and South America as well as importing timber from Scandinavia and North America. Newburgh had ten boats to transport coal alone and was the main shipping port for fish and agricultural produce heading to London from the area. There were also boats bringing in raw materials for weaving from Dundee, pleasure steamers and a ferry from Pow of Errol, not to mention boats travelling to and from Perth harbour.

It would seem that traffic congestion is not a modern phenomenon – the harbour must have been chaotic at times.

Sadly, most of the industries that kept the harbour busy have gone and roads are now the main transport routes. The open area by the river was the site of a linoleum factory until a fire destroyed it in 1980. It has recently been restored into a lovely green space for all to enjoy thanks to the efforts of Newburgh Community Trust and the support of the townspeople. Newburgh is a tremendously active community; Saturday coffee mornings in the Tayside Institute are always packed out and not to be missed if you're in the area.

The Community Trust (www.newburghct.org.uk) is currently looking at ways to restore the harbour piers, which have become unsafe, with a view to making Newburgh a vibrant port once again.

Until the 1920s Mugdrum Island was a small farm growing cereals, potatoes and turnips in the rich soil deposited by the river. Reeds were also gathered and sold for thatching. Nowadays, it is home to fallow deer and sheep that are best seen from further up the hill.

You are now almost at the northern end of the Coastal Path. Turn left and head up West Port Road. Turn right into Mugdrum Park and follow the path uphill to the car park at Mugdrum Park. Your journey is now at an end.

I hope you have enjoyed exploring this unseen corner of Fife and will be back again soon. It takes a bit of persistence to access this part of the countryside but it's well worth it.

There are also some optional loops offering circular walks off this section of the Coastal Path.

The first optional walking loop is from Balmerino Abbey. You have the option of following a path that runs along the coast through Flisk Woods and rejoins the Coastal Path via a field edge just to the west of Thornton Farm. Flisk Woods are the largest and least-disturbed area of mixed deciduous woods in Fife being mostly elm and ash, but with a fine mix of conifers and beech sprinkled among them. In the springtime the woods are carpeted with wild garlic (ramsons) and bluebells and are really beautiful.

The second loop is from Blinkie Strip. The path heads gradually downhill along the bottom of the treelines to Newburgh, but you could choose to turn right here and head downhill through a gate which joins a track through the fields to the coast road. Cross the road and go through a gate leading to steps down into the fields opposite through a series of gates to the sea wall. You can then walk along the bank of the river and come in to Newburgh that way.

Did You Know?
Sea Eagles

With a wingspan extending to a startling eight feet, the white-tailed eagle – or sea eagle as it is better known – is Scotland's largest bird of prey. Yet, in spite of their formidable appearance, the sea eagle had completely disappeared from British soil by the 20th century because of persecution and numbers have only begun to increase following considerable conservation efforts from agencies such as the RSBP and Scottish Natural Heritage.

Most recently, autumn 2011 saw the release of 16 sea eagles from a location in Fife in a further attempt to fully re-establish these beautiful birds throughout Scotland.

Although sightings of sea eagles are still relatively rare, much is known about the species and this valuable information is of particular use in ensuring their successful reintroduction. It may seem in direct contradiction to their name, but the preferred habitat of sea eagles is, surprisingly, not coastal sites, but rather more sheltered locations such as sea lochs or lochs in land.

In Fife, sightings of sea eagles have been made in the areas around Tentsmuir – an area already well-known for its bird life. This non-migratory bird stays close to its favoured breeding locations throughout the year and is thought to venture in the range of just 20 to 40 miles from the site. Significantly, the survival of the sea eagle is hampered by its own habits, as it is thought that up to 70 per cent of young birds of prey do not survive their first winter beyond the nest. This combined with a relatively low rate of reproduction means that even with the right habitats and food sources, survival is a challenging matter.

Sea eagles were once a persecuted species, hunted for sport and because of their perceived threat to smaller livestock. Even now, despite the birds protected status, there are still very real dangers facing the species.

Although it is now relatively rare, egg collecting does continue and cases of poisoning have been recorded as recently as 2003. However, through increased efforts to protect the species, public awareness of sea eagles is also increasing, leading to greater vigilance, particularly in areas where young are nesting. It is hoped that this will have a positive impact and lead to a decline in wildlife crime against the species.

Attempts to reintroduce sea eagles have, until relatively recently been focused on the west coast in Scotland, with a project on the island of Mull among the most notable. However, since 2007 the East Scotland Sea Eagle project has been in place and run in partnership by the RSPB, Scottish Natural Heritage and Forestry Commission Scotland. The project was set up with the aim of establishing a self-sustaining population of white-tailed eagles in East and Central Scotland, as well as ensuring that the people within these regions are given the opportunity to see these birds of prey.

The first group of eagles, 15 in total, were released in August 2007 and the project aims to reach a total of 100 by its conclusion. By the end of 2011, 80 eagles will have been released by the project, having been brought in from Norway, carefully reared and then set free. Each bird is tagged and fitted with a VHF radio in order that staff can track their location and survival from the project and by members of the public too.

As the numbers of released eagles surviving in the wild increases, so too does optimism for the successful reintroduction of the species to Scotland. The ultimate goal, the successful breeding of an eagle chick in the wild, is hoped for as early as 2012 and will give the strongest signal yet that the sea eagle is here to stay.

On behalf of all of us, I hope you have enjoyed your walk along the Fife Coastal Path. If you are feeling energetic, why not try it again in the opposite direction, it's amazing how many other things you will spot if you do. Haste Ye Back!

LOCAL BUSINESSES

NEWBURGH

Food and beverage

East Port Cafe and Garage, Cupar Road, Newburgh, KY14 6HA
Tel: 01337 840379,
Email: ianhennen@live.co.uk

Bite N Blether Café, 94 High Street, Newburgh, KY14 6DA.
Tel: 01337 842906,
Email: alison.batchelor@tiscali.co.uk

Bear Tavern, 47 High Street, Newburgh, KY14 6AH.
Tel: 01337 840365

J & A Scobie Newsagent, 72 High Street, Newburgh, KY14 6AQ.
Tel:01337 840110

The Co-operative, 128-134 High Street, Newburgh, KY14 6DX.
Tel: 01337 840277

The Abbey Inn, High Street, Newburgh, KY14 6EZ.
Tel: 01337 840761

The Tower Bakery, 174 High Street, Newburgh, KY14 6DZ.
Tel: 01337 840491

The Bakery, 108 High Street, Newburgh, KY14 6DA. Tel: 01337 840491. towerbakery.bpweb.net

Sunbo Chinese, 126 High Street, Newburgh, KY14 6DX.
Tel: 01337 840408

Post Office

Key Store, 102 High Street, Newburgh, KY14 6DA. Tel: 01337 840213

Bank

ATM, 89 High Street, Newburgh, KY14 6DA

Arts and Crafts

Sun Gallery, 154 High Street, Newburgh, KY14 6DZ. Tel: 01337 842323, sales@sungallery.co.uk, www.sungallery.co.uk

The Steeple Arts Centre, The Steeple, 67 High Street, Newburgh, KY14 6AH. www.steeplearts.co.uk

Twist Fibre Craft, 88 High Street, Newburgh,KY14 6AQ.
Tel: 01337 842506

THE MARY LEISHMAN FOUNDATION

THE Mary Leishman Foundation was formed in 2009 after the sad loss of a beloved wife, mother and friend. Mary Leishman gave a lifetime of service to all those who knew her, especially being inspirational to the young and old in the Kelty Musical Association. Born and bred in Fife, Mary had great charisma which was natural, she was so down to earth, yet had such class that if she smiled and said hello to you, it would be an uplifting experience – a rare gift given to a chosen few.

The inaugural fundraising event was the `Dander for Mary' along the Fife Coastal Path. A dedicated team of friends, family and acquaintances walked the path not only raising money in Mary's memory but also trying to come to terms with the tragic loss.

This group, three years on is still walking every year aiming to raise funds to support the Mary Leishman Foundation's values of 'Easing Distress and Encouraging Potential', and are now known as the 'Dander Family'. This year,

Mary Leishman - a beloved wife, mother and friend

2012, will see the group walk the Fife Coastal Pathway for the third time, a walk that was a favourite of Mary, Jim and the family.

Since its inception, the Mary Leishman Foundation has, through various fundraising events, raised over £500,000. This level of funding enables The Foundation to ease distress and encourage potential among the many community groups and individuals who have been awarded financial support.

A few worthy causes that have benefited from the work carried out by the foundation are:

NHS FIFE

DONATIONS were made to enable the NHS to purchase a bladder scanner for the orthopaedic department in Queen Margaret Hospital Dunfermline and a baby-cooling-vest for the neonatal unit in the new maternity area within the Victoria Hospital Kirkcaldy.

Caroline Inwood from NHS Fife stated: `Both donations have made a huge impact on the treatment of patients within Fife. The bladder scanner allows staff to make better decisions about when patients require to be catheterised, so reducing the risk of infection; and the baby-cooling vest allows babies to be treated in Fife now instead of being moved to neonatal units in other health boards.

C.L.A.S.P.

THIS is a voluntary organisation that provides advice on living and caring for children with cancer and leukaemia. Each year the foundation provides funding towards a Santa Flight, which is a virtual trip, designed for children too sick to fly.

MUSIC FOR SCHOOLS

EVERY school in Fife is offered the opportunity to nominate a pupil to receive a donation from the Foundation to enable the recipient to further their musical ambition.

This is very often used towards tuition fees or purchase of a musical instrument. This has been an ongoing commitment from the Foundation and is often followed up by further donations to individual pupils.

If you would like to know more about the work carried out by the Foundation visit our website at www.maryleishmanfoundation.com .

Thanks a million.

INDEX